HEYWOOD-WAKEFIELD

Harris Gertz

4880 Lower Valley Road, Atglen, PA 19310 USA

Copyright © 2001 by Harris Gertz
Library of Congress Card Number: 00-111902

All rights reserved. No part of this work may be reproduced or used in any form or by any means—graphic, electronic, or mechanical, including photocopying or information storage and retrieval systems—without written permission from the copyright holder.
"Schiffer," "Schiffer Publishing Ltd. & Design," and the "Design of pen and ink well" are registered trademarks of Schiffer Publishing Ltd.

Designed by Bonnie M. Hensley
Cover design by Bruce M. Waters
Type set in Manzanita/Korinna BT

ISBN: 0-7643-1338-X
Printed in China
1 2 3 4

Published by Schiffer Publishing Ltd.
4880 Lower Valley Road
Atglen, PA 19310
Phone: (610) 593-1777; Fax: (610) 593-2002
E-mail: Schifferbk@aol.com
Please visit our web site catalog at **www.schifferbooks.com**

This book may be purchased from the publisher.
Include $3.95 for shipping. Please try your bookstore first.
We are always looking for people to write books on new and related subjects.
If you have an idea for a book please contact us at the above address.
You may write for a free catalog.

In Europe, Schiffer books are distributed by Bushwood Books
6 Marksbury Avenue Kew Gardens
Surrey TW9 4JF England
Phone: 44 (0) 20-8392-8585; Fax: 44 (0) 20-8392-9876
E-mail: Bushwd@aol.com
Free postage in the UK. Europe: air mail at cost.

Preface

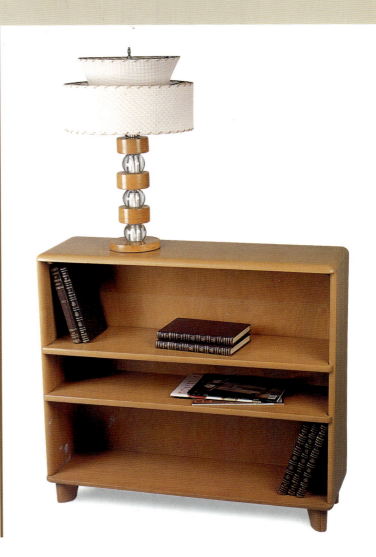

This book deals exclusively with Heywood-Wakefield modern design solid blond maple and birch furniture produced from 1936 to 1966. It represents only a segment of the various residential, commercial, and institutional lines of furniture made by Heywood-Wakefield, which existed as a family-owned company from 1826 to 1983. The long and complex company history that predates the introduction of what is, by far, their most collectable line of goods, will not be explored here. What will be presented is an in-depth survey of the style trends and other related factors concerning their Modern Line. Many of the conclusions herein are opinions based on the author's years of hands-on specialization in buying, selling, and restoring this furniture, and an even broader, general background in having grown up in the antique furniture business. Specific information regarding design credit and years of production for each piece of furniture is taken from company literature, including original sales catalogs, promotional brochures, and company newsletters, and from interviews with former Heywood-Wakefield employees and their relatives.

Since several sales catalogs are missing, dates of production and design attribution of some items are educated estimates drawn from many years of handling thousands of pieces of Heywood-Wakefield Modern. Dimensions have been taken almost entirely from the actual pieces. The items photographed in this book are taken from the author's own company inventory and generous additions from a few enthusiastic collector/dealers and customers. The furniture pictured does not represent the entire Heywood-Wakefield Modern Line, but is a comprehensive cross-section of the best styles.

The intent here is to take the appreciation of Heywood-Wakefield to a higher level.

Finally, many of the photographs show the furniture from different angles and some in actual room settings. Hopefully, this will provide some of the same enjoyment as seeing the furniture in person.

Acknowledgments

Special thanks to Sam Camhe of *Mostly Modern*, Chris Parody *of Strictly Heywake*, Peter Gertz, John and Diane Vitale, Audrey Manley, *Radical Media*, Nick Hemmerich, David Hester, Bob Rossiter, and Trudy Brady for allowing their pieces to be photographed so that a well-rounded out book could be assembled. Special thanks also to Pam Meitzler at the Levi Heywood Memorial Library in Gardner, Massachusetts, for her gracious help, and for allowing the original Heywood-Wakefield sales catalogs to be photographed.

Tremendous thanks to Sandy Forrest for her vital assistance in writing and arranging the text and photographs. Thanks also to Steve Gertz and Paula Attanasio for their help with the physical rigors of the photography.

Contents

1. Introduction 6
2. Collecting Heywood-Wakefield 9
   Finish and Restoration 10
   Indentification 12
   Pricing 12
3. Bedrooms 16
4. Dining Rooms 55
5. Living Rooms 102
6. Utility Pieces 138
Price Guide 158

1. Introduction

What is good furniture? What are the specific criteria by which we can evaluate furniture in order to establish overall merit? Good furniture must plainly exhibit four major characteristics or else in some way be considered inferior. They are: style, function, durability, and affordability.

There is no denying that style matters. While it is the most subjective of the aforementioned qualities, style is what catches the eye and usually leads to closer inspection of the piece of furniture in terms of other qualities. Good furniture must look good. However, appearance only goes so far. Quality furniture must be useful. It must do what it is supposed to do and look good at the same time. Once these two qualities are united in a piece of furniture what follows next in importance is durability. What good is stylish, functional furniture if it is not durable enough to get your money's worth? Finally, none of this matters if an otherwise terrific item is unaffordable. While any of these four criteria can vary in importance to a given consumer, it is often hard to find good furniture that embodies all four.

Heywood-Wakefield's streamlined, solid birch and maple modern furniture, produced from 1936 to 1966, fits all of these criteria. Its relative abundance compared to furniture made by other mid-century modern furniture manufacturers is testimony to its quality on a piece-by-piece basis, as well as to the success of the company. What was true during Heywood-Wakefield's production of their modern line is true now—good looking, useful, well-made, and affordable furniture is bound to be popular. Though contrary to the idea in collecting antiques that rarity is equated with value, abundance may actually be the best barometer of worth when it comes to practical things like vintage furniture.

"Heywood-Wakefield was the first American manufacturer to produce modern furniture in sizable quantity…the first American manufacturer to recognize modern as a definitive, lasting period of design." From the 1938 Heywood-Wakefield catalog

For Heywood-Wakefield's durability we must acknowledge the people who built the furniture. However, who is responsible for designing it and shaping its 30-year style evolution? Gilbert Rohde designed some veneered walnut furniture for Heywood Wakefield prior to 1936 and is also credited with a few blond maple designs issued after his departure to Herman Miller.

Industrial designers Count Alexis de Sakhnoffsky, Leo Jiranek, Alfons Bach, and Joseph Carr are also mentioned in company literature for their design contributions. Prior to World War II, Sakhnoffsky or Jiranek medallions were put on the bedroom pieces they designed, usually placed in the top drawer of a chest. Since these medallions are so hard to find now, it is unclear whether they were used in limited situations or if they are simply missing so often from the pieces they belonged to. After World War II, Carr collaborated on designs with Ernest Herman and Frank Parrish, though they weren't credited on the pieces. Except for Gilbert Rohde, these are not household names, yet the designers' genius is obvious in the individual pieces and in their collective effort of creating an enduring 30-year-long line.

Hindsight is valuable in terms of appreciating the 30-year style evolution of Heywood-Wakefield furniture. Looked at from a historical perspective, furniture made of solid American wood had to be quite attractive for anyone to invest in it during the Depression. The clean, uncomplicated, and stylish designs were instantly appealing to the public as Heywood-Wakefield's sales grew despite hard times. The simple lines were refreshing; they were forward thinking and borrowed very little from previous styles. The blond color, combined with the graceful lines, enabled Heywood-Wakefield to market their streamlined modern line as sunny and pleasant to live with. Also, the scale of the pieces were relatively small, making it ideally suited for modern (i.e. smaller) living spaces during hard times. Functionally speaking, most Heywood-Wakefield pieces are fully usable as they waste little space. For example, most dressers of other, earlier furniture styles sit on fairly tall legs. Most Heywood-Wakefield dressers extend close to the floor, using more of the floor space they occupy. In addition, the new concept of modular furniture incorporated sectional seating, uniform storage components, and drop-leaf tables into their Modern Line, as making the most of a space was one of the company's central design concepts.

"Because it follows no stilted or stodgy period rules…because it does not have to imitate anything from the past; Modern can be designed with originality…with an eye for utility and adaptability, as well as beauty." From the 1940 Heywood-Wakefield catalog.

Heywood-Wakefield designs from the 1930s until the beginning of World War II exhibit the classic streamlined modern look. The long, bent, solid-wood stretchers beneath tables and the curved fronts of case pieces illustrate this best as do the rounded edges that are perhaps the most recognizable feature of all Heywood-Wakefield designs. Streamlining was the style of the 1930s in America and Heywood-Wakefield's ability to steam-bend solid wood put them at the forefront of furniture design during that era. The added advantage Heywood-Wakefield had was the development of blond finishes, which gave their furniture a brighter look than the darker, Art Deco pieces offered by contemporary manufacturers. This brightness conveys an informality that was a constant attribute in Heywood-Wakefield furniture as the designs evolved. Its warmth also would set it apart from the austere, architecturally spare furniture simultaneously produced by Knoll and Herman Miller in the 1940s and 1950s.

"In 1937 Heywood-Wakefield developed a light, modern finish which was named WHEAT. This finish, which suggests the lovely tones of natural, ripened grains, became an overnight sensation. WHEAT brought to Modern the one remaining quality it needed…the charm and character of a lively color." From the 1940 catalog.

There was a period of about three years during World War II during which Heywood-Wakefield put less effort into bending woods or rounding edges on many pieces. It is almost tempting to ignore this segment of time, for it added very little to design evolution, though the quality of construction, function, and affordability were still maintained. Furniture production was accordingly low during this time, so these pieces that lack some of the characteristic Heywood-Wakefield streamlined style are rare. This, incidentally, is a case where rarity means nothing in terms of desirability to today's collectors.

By the post-war era, while Heywood-Wakefield's designs could still be considered streamlined given their inherent simplicity and curvaceous lines, they started showing signs of biomorphism that foretold of a more 1950s look. Organic shapes were prevalent in many of their best designs from this period. Legs on cabinets, occasional tables, dining tables, and chairs resemble spider and centipede legs. Handles on dressers and cabinets became sensuous and shapely–almost asking to be touched. Many of their best items from this era also convey an atomic look that is representative of the times. Post-war prosperity combined with Heywood-Wakefield's seductively appealing designs, made the late 1940s to mid-1950s their most productive period. To meet the increased demand, sales catalogs from this period offered more choices compared to previous years.

By the latter half of the 1950s the company started introducing some thinner-edged pieces. These items were indicative of the final design shift in the furniture's evolution. The lines became a bit sharper and some of the organic, curvaceous elements were dropped. Even though quality was not sacrificed, these design changes in some cases may have helped cut costs as production declined. For example, some legs on chairs and tables that were introduced around 1950 became thinner by the late 1950s. Although some of the pieces can be quite elegantly appealing, round, rather than sharp lines, were more characteristic of Heywood-Wakefield's over all look.

From the 1939 catalog.

Special silver-plated signature medallion reads, "Designed by Leo Jiranek, Rockefeller Center"

This 1944 catalog was actually a fold-open poster showing a limited, wartime menu of available items. Notice the very utilitarian design of the Victory group.

2. Collecting Heywood-Wakefield

Around 1980 some people rediscovered Heywood-Wakefield because it was affordable used furniture that had style and integrity. It was at this time that many of the homes originally furnished with Heywood-Wakefield were either being redecorated for the next generation or their occupants relocated or died. That led to an initial wave of Heywood-Wakefield being released onto the secondary market. Over the next 20 years the progression of its availability went from junk and Salvation Army stores, to general antiques stores which showed a piece occasionally, to shops that specialized in it exclusively. This, by the way, is the sequence of events that many types of furniture follow provided they are stylish enough to command attention the second time around and are well-built enough to last. Furthermore, as interest in Heywood-Wakefield has grown, and it has steadily grown over the past 20 years, the values have also risen. In spite of this, Heywood-Wakefield is still reasonably priced compared to newly made furniture of similar quality and downright affordable compared to many of its mid-century contemporaries that have been simultaneously rediscovered. In addition to value for the dollar, Heywood-Wakerfield's resurgent popularity can be credited to its unpretentiousness. It was never designed to be furniture sold as art.

The relative abundance of Heywood-Wakefield furniture is a blessing for the person interested in collecting or furnishing with it. The thrill of the hunt is a fun concept when collecting some things, however it is a luxury to have immediate choices when it comes to functional furniture. Because Heywood-Wakefield's Modern Line was so extensive, today's consumer has many options. A prospective buyer of Heywood-Wakefield in 1950, for example, had only two bedroom sets and five dining room chair styles to choose from. Today one can stand back and examine 30 years worth of goods before making a selection. This is not to suggest that every piece they produced is available at any one time or place, though there are several antique shops across the country that offer consistently large inventories. Also, considering that most vintage Heywood-Wakefield has lasted at least 40 years so far, one can buy with the confidence that they are investing in durable merchandise that has stood the test of time. That it continues to appreciate in value is a bonus.

The 1950 wholesale price list.

From the 1941 catalog.

Finish and Restoration

It makes no sense to discuss value without first taking into account the color and condition of the finish. First, the fact that Heywood-Wakefield furniture is only 50 or 60 years old immediately creates an expectation that it should be clean, if not perfect. Wear and tear is not considered acceptable as it is on older furniture of other styles. Perhaps Heywood-Wakefield will always be held to a stricter standard than other antique furniture because it has modern, clean lines and a light-colored finish. A cigarette burn or a water ring, for example, are major eyesores on a blond finish, more so than on a dark piece of furniture. Heywood-Wakefield is the opposite of rustic. It is rather like a vintage automobile, in that a scratch never gives it more character.

Heywood-Wakefield finished their maple and birch in a variety of blond colors and a few that were stained dark brown. By far the best and most common finishes are Wheat and Champagne.

For the serious collector, those are only two colors that matter. It must be noted that there was appreciable variation in the original wheat and champagne finishes. Champagne particularly evolved from a mostly orange-amber tone in the 1940s to showing hints of pink in its orange hue in the 1950s. By the late 1950s, Champagne was more overtly pink. These three versions of Champagne do not match each other exactly, although they are all original. Wheat tended to be more consistent, though its subtle changes can be traced from an earlier, lighter, slightly whitish yellow, to a more golden yellow after World War II and into the 1950s. By the late 1950s, Wheat had evolved into an icier yellow with an almost greenish cast. The effects of age, sunlight, air and cigarette smoke on these finishes create even more subtle variety in what we see when we observe Heywood-Wakefield finishes today. Other original finishes were Amber, Bleached, and Walnut prior to World War II, and Platinum, Mellow Birch, Tampico, Westwood, Topaz, Sable, Priscilla, Clove, Fruitwood, Sherry, and Monticello after World War II. In addition to Wheat and Champagne, only Amber, Bleached, Platinum, Mellow Birch and Tampico are finishes that are blond enough to be considered in character with the informal style of Heywood-Wakefield. They are so uncommon, though, that it would make no sense to start collecting pieces in those colors with the hope of finding very much of it. As for the various brown finishes, they are so out of character with the style of the furniture that the color significantly devalues the piece. For example, a piece that has an original, mint condition, Sable finish has less value than the identical piece in Wheat in extremely poor condition. The Sable piece would require more extensive effort to restore it to a desirable Wheat finish than restoring the distressed Wheat piece.

It would be easier to place a value on Heywood Wakefield if it were all in original, mint condition instead of being in varying degrees of distress. However, it is very rare to find a piece that is perfect. Most pieces are found needing some or total restoration work. Some pieces are clean over all, but may have one fatal scratch or gouge. Some are clean except for a section such as an over all clean dresser with a worn top. Other pieces have a finish that is completely dried and flaking off and occasionally some have certain structural damage. This leads to the subject of restoration.

Because so few pieces of Heywood Wakefield furniture have survived in mint original condition (and considering the aforementioned standards which blond furniture is held to), restoration of the pieces is *mandatory* to satisfy the growing market and *necessary* to elevate most items to their full value. The few buyers and dealers who may consider restoration unacceptable have probably never seen it done correctly. It is generally accepted as very difficult to accurately reproduce the original Heywood-Wakefield finish. The critical point is that restoration is acceptable ONLY if done properly—and it is rarely done properly. *The proper finish should look like the original factory finish.* This means achieving the correct color, gloss, and opacity. There should be enough grain coverage so that uneven grains do not visually distract from the overall lines of the furniture, yet enough clarity so that the item does not look painted. This is the only way to restore any piece to its full value. Since exactly duplicating a 50-year old finish can be nearly impossible, the more a restored piece blends in with original pieces, the more competent the restoration job. For this reason, clear, colorless finishes do nothing to enhance the value of Heywood-Wakefield.

From the point of view of having sold a great deal of Heywood-Wakefield, a properly restored piece is worth more than a piece with the original finish that has a few minor flaws. Subtle signs of wear and use go a long way in lowering Heywood-Wakefield's value. Depending on severity, a scratch can be expertly touched up or a section of a piece can be redone to match the rest of the item, but this can take more skill than restoring the entire piece. On the other hand, an improperly refinished piece can be worth as little or less than a dirty, original piece depending on how it was done. Undoing misguided workmanship can be harder than restoring a distressed original finish. At times structural problems, such as boards separating at their joints, can lower a piece's value. (A tabletop is usually several pieces of wood joined together). Rarely are there problems, however, that cannot be fixed. If you can find a craftsman or an antique dealer who can artistically repair a hurt piece with the necessary integrity, then you can elevate it to its full value. That Heywood-Wakefield is repairable and restorable is due largely to the fact that it was solid wood and well-made in the first place.

Putting aside considerations of color or restoration, style is an even more critical factor in determining the value of a piece. Between two M154 chairs, the cleaner one is obviously worth more. However, not every mint piece is valuable because style needs to be considered. A mint M553 chair is not worth as much as a M154 chair that needs work because the M553 is not as sought-after as the M154. Condition, critical as it may be, never trumps style.

The value of Heywood Wakefield upholstered furniture varies radically according to condition. Obviously, original, mint condition fabric, although nearly impossible to find, is a wonderful thing. Upholstered pieces that have wear, tears, stains, discoloration, or deterioration or have been poorly reupholstered, are only worth the value of the frame since the expense of reupholstering can match or exceed the worth of the item. Some upholstered pieces, especially Aristocraft, show significant amounts of wood. These must be evaluated by the condition of the finish of the wood as well as the status of the fabric.

From the point of view of having sold a great deal of this furniture, original fabric is not always a barometer of worth, although being original it may evoke historical interest. What good is a clean, original red sofa if one's color scheme is green? A piece that has been reupholstered in desirable fabric can have more worth to a buyer than the same piece with mint, original, but undesired, upholstery. Value often depends on what the consumer wants.

From the 1940 catalog.

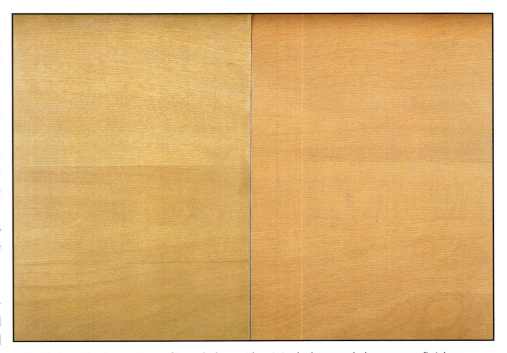

A side-by-side comparison of two shelves with original wheat and champagne finishes. They were described by Heywood-Wakefield as follows: "WHEAT is a yellow cast that resembles the color of ripened wheat grain. CHAMPAGNE is a pink tone that resembles the color of a correctly-made Champagne cocktail."

The top of this Encore M518 night stand has black water stains and large bald spots. It will be a challenge to restore.

Here are two M155 chairs: The one on the right is stripped to bare wood and the one on the left has been restored. This clearly shows how the proper Heywood-Wakefield finish de-emphasizes the variation in the color and grain of the individual boards that make up a chair back. A clear finish applied to the stripped chair would actually <u>accentuate</u> the unsightly juxtaposition of mismatched boards, distracting the eye from the overall lines of the chair.

Identification

Heywood-Wakefield Modern is fairly easy to identify, if not by its distinctive styling, then by their various labels and markings. Pieces produced prior to 1946 had glued-on paper labels. Although those labels sometimes deteriorated or fell off, the items can still be identified by a stamp, on the back or underneath, of the finish color and style number—a letter C followed by four numbers. Items produced after World War II had the company logo either branded in a top drawer or ink-stamped on the back or underneath along with the color and style number—a letter M followed by three or four numbers. Dates can be found on post-war items only although the tiny digits are frequently illegible.

Pricing

The values given for the furniture in this book are based on professional experience. Since there is no foolproof way to place an exact value on an antique item due to regional preferences and fluctuating demand the numbers may vary due to time and place. Considering that the overwhelming majority of surviving Heywood-Wakefield pieces need restoration, **the values given in this book are for items in fair condition.** One can expect to pay substantially more, though, for mint or professionally restored pieces. On the other hand, items that are extremely distressed due to human or environmental abuse are worth less than the outlined prices. Of even less value still are pieces with structural damages, such as broken parts, missing pieces, warped boards, or joint separation, or items that have been painted or stained dark. Included in this category are china closets with broken or missing glass doors, and vanities or dressers with broken or chipped mirrors. Upholstered items are valued as if they require recovering, since they almost always do.

Finally, it is something of a paradox that rarity is not always a factor when evaluating Heywood-Wakefield furniture. Certain items are scarce because they were never popular styles in the first place. Some items are scarce because they were made in the less prolific years during World War II. This does not increase value. On the other hand, some of the most heavily produced pieces are still the most desirable—quite often what was good then is good now. This is not to suggest that there aren't some rare pieces that have value, like the M395 record cabinet. Stated simply, though, style is frequently a better barometer of value than rarity.

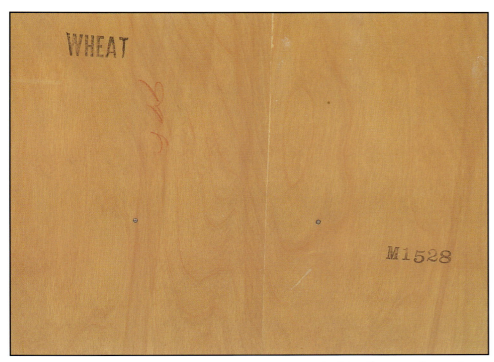

The style number and color are clearly stamped on the back of this Encore night stand. Sometimes the effects of aging and environment obscure these markings.

The rear of this Niagara chest has a glued-on paper label accompanied by the style number. This red, white, and blue label was used up until World War II.

The bottom of this upholstered bench bears a clear date of production.

This wood-grained paper label was also used on early pieces, although it may have been discontinued after 1939.

The tag pictured here was affixed to early upholstered items. In addition to the style number and color it had a fabric code indicating to the factory upholsterers which material was to be used.

Almost all items produced after World War II bear the eagle logo.

By state law, furniture makers were required to indicate on upholstered furniture that the fabric was brand new and to list the materials used to stuff the item.

Upholstered pieces produced after World War II usually had a silk label stitched on them.

The reverse side gives instructions for caring for the finely finished furniture.

This tasseled cardboard medallion, boasting the DuPont finish that Heywood-Wakefield used, was secured to various pieces by furniture retailers. It is rarely seen and may only have been used on floor samples.

3. Bedrooms

What sets Heywood-Wakefield bedroom furniture apart from the pieces they built for other rooms is the fact that they were designed in matched suites. Although these pieces were available individually, specific design elements tie together dressers, beds, vanities, and nightstands. In contrast, there were more mix-and-match options when purchasing dining room sets. Certainly one can put together a mix-and-match bedroom suite today with items from different years, but usually a matched suite, as the designers intended, looks best in a bedroom.

An interesting trend occurred in the 1950s towards introducing more options into the bedroom set lines. The Encore group had by far the most choices. Dressers of varying widths and heights were available, as were two different night tables and three different vanities. Bedrooms prior to 1948 did not offer this much variety within the style. Since the Encore and Sculptura lines were in production for the longest time it was in the company's interest to offer the most options in those styles. Plus, these styles were produced during Heywood-Wakefield's most prolific years. This has increased their current availability. Interestingly, the fact that they are more commonly available does not make them less desirable now.

In terms of style evolution, there were several design changes among bedroom pieces that took place over time. Earlier or pre-war dressers tended to have a more rounded appearance achieved by steam bending the fronts of drawers. This can be likened to the curvaceous automobiles of the era. Not coincidentally, Count Alexis de Sakhoffsky, one of Heywood Wakefield's chief designers in the 1930s also designed cars for Chrysler. Other features of most earlier dressers were the platform bases that sat on the floor (as opposed to having legs) and pulls that were positioned down the centers of the drawers giving the pieces an overall streamlined look. The Niagara dressers illustrate all three of these features.

After the war, steam bending the drawer fronts was no longer done, although drawer design became no less interesting. The concave/convex drawer fronts of Kohinoor or the ribbon-like fronts of Sculptura are quite engaging to look at and function well as handles. Encore's flat front cases are more subtly appealing as the drawers flow effortlessly into the sides of the case. The long, lip-like handles accentuate the simplicity of the design. It is interesting that a big part of what gave Encore, and particularly Kohinoor, their 1950s flair are the little feet they stood on. Encore had small, oval, tapered feet and Kohinoor had spidery, splayed legs. Although these may seem like minor details, they were important to the over all look.

In terms of construction, Heywood Wakefield's dressers were very well put together. Remove all of the drawers and one can see a structural framework of dividers that section off the interior of the case. It seems a given fact that a quality piece of furniture would be built that well. However, dressers built by other prominent furniture companies, including those with designer pedigrees like Herman Miller, were often a frameless box of air behind the drawers. Heywood Wakefield may seem almost over-built by comparison, but the result is drawers that almost always pull out smoothly. This is impressive in 50-year-old furniture.

Note: each item is captioned with its style number, dimensions, dates of production and designer, if applicable.

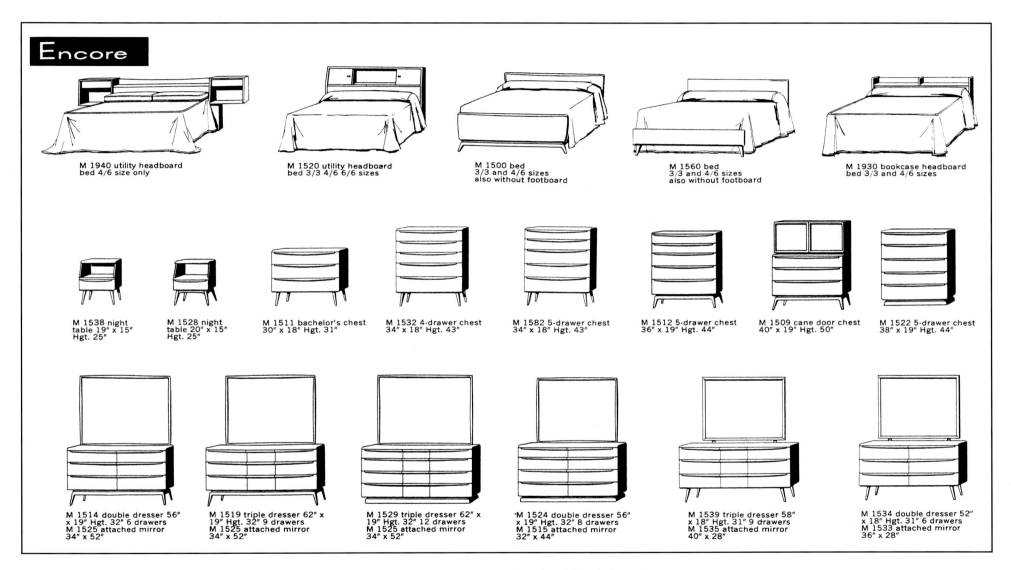

A chart of Encore pieces available in the 1958–1959 catalog.

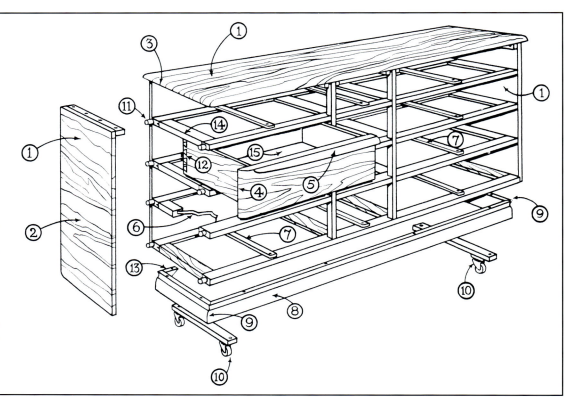

1. All exposed parts are solid Northern Birch selected and matched for color.
2. Ends are constructed with horizontal grain to permit climatic expansion and contraction and prevent drawer binding or sticking.
3. Top edges are rounded and sanded to present soft flowing lines.
4. Drawer fronts are individually custom sanded and fitted to each case to insure finger-tip movement.
5. Solid wood pulls are shaped and tapered and individually fitted to each drawer.
6. Entire case is fully dustproofed with hard-board panels fitted into frame rails.
7. All drawers are center guided for easy movement.
8. Heavy base is shaped and sanded.
9. Base is mitered and corner blocked at front corners for extra strength and rigidity.
10. All bedroom cases fitted with four ball bearing swivel casters.
11. Mortised and tenoned frame rail interior construction for continuing rigidity.
12. All drawers are custom fitted and feature lasting dovetail construction.
13. Rear corner brace assures rugged strength.
14. End frame rail fitted between front and rear rails with Heywood-Wakefield floating frame construction which allows for expansion and contraction of solid Birch.
15. Drawer interiors finished and waxed to hold the most delicate fabrics.

The construction of an Encore Mrs. and Mrs. dresser is shown in the 1964–1965 catalog.

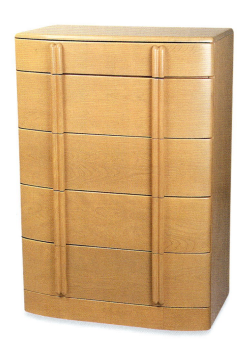

Airflow Chest
C3332
32"w x 19"d x 46"h
1937–1939
Designer: Leo Jiranek
One of Heywood-Wakefield's most dramatic designs, it has an almost architectural look.
$400–600

C3332 Detail
Top drawer was fitted with a shirt partition. Many highboys had this feature.

Airflow Dresser
C3331
42"w x 20"d x 34"h
Designer: Leo Jiranek
1937–1939
$350-550

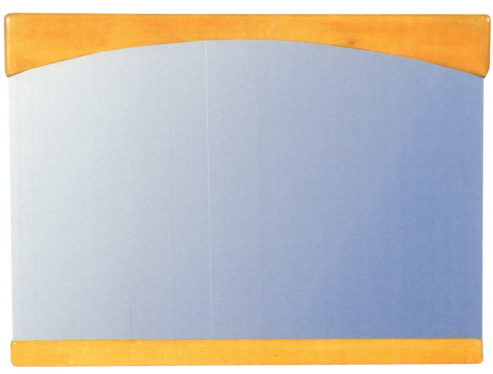

Airflow Mirror
C3333
34"w x 22"h
Designer: Leo Jiranek
1937–1939

Airflow Nightstand
C3338
14"w x 14"d x 25.5"h
1937–1939
A very simple complement to a great bedroom set.
$150-200

The 1937 catalog showing:
Airflow Vanity
C3340
52"w x 18"d x 22"h
60.5" over all height
Designer: Leo Jiranek
1937–1939
$400-600

Airflow Bed
C3330
Available in twin or full sizes
1937–1939
Designer: Leo Jiranek
Notice how the footboard wrapped around the corners of the bed. This created a streamlined look that was available on only a few early beds.
$200-300

**Skyliner Nightstand
C3568**
14"w x 14"d x 25.5"h
1939–1940
A very futuristic style.
$150-200

C3568 Detail
Notice how the drawer handle appears connected to the upright leg.

**Skyliner Chest
C3562**
32"w x 19"d x 45"h
1939–1940
An innovative modern design with vertically aligned handles that flow visually into unusual feet, giving the chest a floating appearance.
$350-550

Blanket Chest
C3739
40"w x 14"d x 17.5"h
1940–1942
A useful item, this chest is extremely hard to find. The upholstered lid has the original fabric.
$500-700

C3739 Detail
The lid is also upholstered on the inside.

Niagara Chest
C3922
33"w x 20"d x 47"h
1941–1942
Designer: Leo Jiranek
The classic streamlined look: bow front drawers, centered handles, and recessed platform.
$400-600

Niagara Dresser with Mirror
C3921-923
42"w x 20"d x 34"h
Mirror: C3923
40" x 28"
1941–1942
Designer: Leo Jiranek
$350-550

Niagara Vanity Seat
C3927
20"w x 17"h
1941–1942
Designer: Leo Jiranek
One of the sweetest vanity stools made, featuring a revolving channel-stitched seat with a unique backrest. The original floral fabric is in excellent condition.
$150-200

Niagara Vanity
C3926
53"w x 18"d x 23"h
61" over all height
1941–1942
Designer: Leo Jiranek
Two elegantly curved drawer pedestals flank a glass shelf and a full-length mirror–a prime example of the extra design focus placed on the vanity within a bedroom set.
$450-550

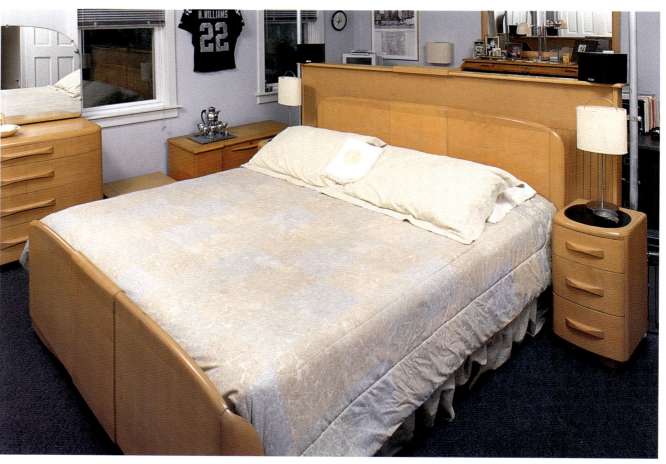

Niagara Bed
C3920
Available in twin or full sizes
1941–1942
Designer: Leo Jiranek
Recently redesigned example of a C3920 bed with a center panel added to expand from full to king size. Also shown; C3928 Niagara nightstand, 14"w x 14"d x 25.5"h, 1941–1942.
Bed: $200-300; nightstand, $175-275

**Mirror
C3915**
32" x 26"
Detail
Mirror adjusts to the correct viewing height.

**Miami Chest
C3912**
32"w x 19"d x 43"h
1941–1942
Designer: Leo Jiranek
The perfect set for a small room. The highboy has four drawers instead of five. The dresser has three drawers instead of four.
$400-500

**Miami Dresser with Mirror
C3911-915**
42"w x 19"d x 34"h
1941–1942
Designer: Leo Jiranek
$300-400

C3916, C3917

Miami Vanity
C3916
46"w x 18"d x 23"h
56" over all height
1941–1942
Designer: Leo Jiranek
A dressing table offers the luxury of extra drawer space and a large mirror in a bedroom.
$400-500

**Miami Vanity Bench
C3917**
24"l x 15"w x 17"h
1941–1942
Designer: Leo Jiranek
$100-150

**Miami Nightstand
C3918**
14"w x 13"d x 25.5"h
1941–1942
Designer: Leo Jiranek
$150-200

C3918 Detail
The bottom is a compartment,
although it appears to be a drawer.

Miami Bed
C3910
Available in twin and full sizes
1941–1942
Designer: Leo Jiranek
$200-300

Rio Dresser with Mirror
C3791-795
42"w x 20"d x 34"h
Mirror: C3795
32" x 34"
1943–1944
Designer: Leo Jiranek
A round mirror is quite uncommon above a Heywood-Wakefield dresser.
$350-450

Rio Chest
C3792
32"w x 19"d x 45"h
1943–1944
Designer: Leo Jiranek
The molded front resembled the sleek automobiles of the era.
$450-550

**Rio Nightstand
C3798**
13"w x 13"d x 25.5"h
1943–1944
Designer: Leo Jiranek
$150-200

**Riviera Nightstand
M188**
13"w x 13"d x 25.5"h
1947–1948
$150-200

**Riviera Chest
M182**
32"w x 19"d x 45"h
1947–1948
This first bedroom set that Heywood-Wakefield produced after World War II was basically a redesign of the Rio set. Centered handles gave Riviera a throw-back look to the pre-war designs. It was the last of this style.
$450-550

M188 Detail
The hinged door on the bottom does not appear on later nightstands.

Encore 5-Drawer Chest
M522
34"w x 19"d x 46"h
1948–1955
Heywood-Wakefield's most popular item in it's most popular bedroom set. Simplicity goes a long way.
$400-600

Encore 4-Drawer Chest
M512
32"w x 19"d x 42"h
1948–1950
A junior-sized highboy for a small space or when four deep drawers are preferable to five slimmer ones.
$350-550

Encore Triple Dresser with Mirror
M529-575
60"w x 19"d x 34"h
1952–1955
Mirror: M575
50" x 34"
A great hard-to-find dresser. Its twelve drawers, including the four small center ones, made it the most functional dresser available. Cutout center handles added whimsical flavor to the simple Encore design. The triple dresser extended the range of bedroom set options.
$700-900

Encore Triple Dresser with Mirror
M1529-1525
62"w x 19"d x 32"h
Mirror: M1525
52" x 34"
1956–1966
The Encore line, redesigned in 1956, offered the option of a platform base on dressers that hid ball bearing casters for easy moving. Handles were redesigned to look continuous across the entire front.
$700-900

**Encore Mr. and Mrs. Dresser with Mirror
M524–575**
54"w x 19"d x 34"h
1948–1955
This extremely popular item, introduced as a bedroom set option after World War II, was designed for sharing.
$500-700

**Encore Mr. and Mrs. Dresser
M1514**
56"w x 19"d x 32"h
1956–1966
The redesigned Encore line featured both an eight-drawer Mr. and Mrs. Dresser with a platform base and this six-drawer dresser with tapered splayed legs.
$450-650

M1514 Detail
Characteristic of Heywood-Wakefield's attention to detail was the sliding jewelry tray in the top drawer of many dressers.

Encore 4-Drawer Dresser
M521
42"w x 19"d x 34"h
1948–1955
This style was also available as the M511 three drawer dresser with the same over all dimensions, but with deeper drawers.
$350-550

Encore Double Chest
M532
44"w x 19"d x 46"h
1954–1955

One of the most functional bedroom pieces designed by Heywood-Wakefield. This chest had the width of a dresser and the height of a tall chest. Produced in very small numbers, as a costly, top-of-the-line option within the Encore group.
$900-1100

M532 Detail
The interior of all Heywood-Wakefield's chests, dressers, and other case furniture with drawers were fitted with dust dividers between each drawer. Any dust created by sliding a drawer in and out could not fall into the contents of the drawer beneath it.

Encore Dresser with Tambour Utility Deck
M1536 on M1521
39.5"w x 17"d x 19"h–top
42"w x 19"d x 32"h–base
51" over all height
1956
Extremely rare deck top adds an extra dimension to a dresser and provides useful enclosed shelf space. Can be used as an entertainment unit to hold a stereo or small TV.
$650-850

M1536 on M1521 Detail
One of the luxuries of tambour doors is simply that they don't take up any space when opened.

**Encore Utility Case
M523**
30"w x 19"d x 34"h
1948–1954
Harder to find than the more standard-sized dressers, this scaled-down chest works great in a small guest room or child's room.
$325-425

**Encore Vanity
M536**
1950–1953
54"w x 18"d x 24"h
65"over all height with mirror
The M536 followed the precedent set by the Kohinoor vanity for asymmetry. The mirror is extended nearly to the floor affording a full-length view. Also shown: M777 Sculptura stool.
$400-600

M536 Detail
Notice the wedge shape of the base. Unusual angles were an interesting part of several Heywood-Wakefield designs after World War II. The glass shelf is useful for perfumes and nail polish which could damage the finish of a wood surface.

**Encore Nightstand
M538**
20"w x 16"d x 26"h
1950–1955
A large, functional bedside table with a futuristic-looking top tier.
$200-275

**Encore Nightstand
M518**
15"w x 14"d x 26"h
1948–1955
This nightstand, narrower than the M538, works better in tighter spaces. The interior shelf is adjustable.
$150-200

Encore Nightstand
M1528
20"w x 15"d x 25"h
1956–1966
After 1956, the trend to make furniture legs narrower is reflected in these slim, tapered legs.
$150-200

Encore Nightstand/Pier Cabinet
M1518
22"w x 17"d x 26"h
1956
More drawer space was provided than in conventional night stands although the enameled metal knobs were not in keeping with the Encore style.
$175-250

Encore Blanket Chest with Mirror
M539-575X
35"w x 15.5"d x 14"h
64" over all height
Mirror: M575X (X suffix indicated vertical mirror attachment to case)
50" x 34"
1952–1953
A rare and unusual item which was available with or without a mirror. Without the mirror it works at the foot of a bed or under a low window.
$600-800

M539-575X Detail
Not a typical blanket chest, it is actually a drawer.

Encore Bed
M510
Available in twin and full sizes
1948–1953
Encore simplicity–the footboard has the cute, oval feet that match dressers and nightstands.
$200-300

Encore Vanity Bench
M587
31"l x 25"w x 15"h
1953
A nice, sizable bench that could also work as an ottoman.
$150-200

Encore Vanity Bench
M537
26"l x 17"w x 15"h
1950–1953
A comfortable bench that can also be used as an ottoman, seen here in the original tufted fabric.
$175-250

Encore Bed and Nightstand
M530
M518
Available in twin and full sizes
1950–1953
One of Heywood-Wakefield's single best designs–
now known as a "dog bone" bed–is very hard to
find. Also shown: M518 nightstand.
Bed: $500-700; nightstand, $150-200

M530 Detail
The fun and informality of Heywood-Wakefield
furniture is clearly expressed in the dog bone cutout.
A standout design!

The cover of the 1950 catalog.

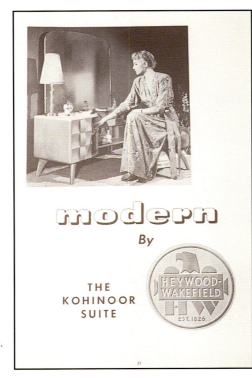

From the 1950 catalog.

Kohinoor Chest
M142
34"w x 19"d x 45"h
1949-1951
The Kohinoor line offered a sharper, more geometric style than previous bedroom sets. The three section drawer front featured concave outside panels and a convex center that served as the handle. Its tapered legs lifted it off the floor more than any previous Heywood-Wakefield bedroom pieces. It was a radical departure from the more rounded, streamlined look of the past.
$400-600

Kohinoor Mr. and Mrs. Dresser
M144–525
56"w x 19"d x 32.5"h
Mirror: M525
40" x 28"
1949–1951
The repetition of the diamond-like drawers is visually engaging.
$500-700

Kohinoor 3-Drawer Dresser with Mirror
M141-145
44"w x 19"d x 32.5"h
Mirror: M145
36"w x 28"h
1949–1951
$300-500

**Kohinoor Vanity
M146**
50"w x 18"d x 23"h
58" over all height
1949–1951
One of Heywood-Wakefield's more stylish bedroom pieces, it was the first of five asymmetrical vanities. It featured a tambour door compartment next to three drawers on the left and two glass shelves on the right. The asymmetrical base tapered from 23" deep on the left to 14" deep on the right.
$450-650

M146 with M537 Stool

**Kohinoor 3-Drawer Dresser with Deck Top
M149 on M141**
42"w x 17.5"d x 10"h–top
44"w x 19"d x 42.5"h–bottom
1949–1951
Though not as many choices were available as in the Encore group, the Kohinoor line included the first chest-on-chest–a two drawer unit atop a three drawer dresser. It was one of the most attractive bedroom pieces the company made. Notice how the top unit is slanted back in keeping with the angularity of the style.
$650-850

Kohinoor Vanity Stool
M147
20"diam. x 17"h
1949–1951
The revolving spider-leg stool harmonizes well with the leggy Kohinoor design.
$150-200

Kohinoor Vanity/Desk
M546
50"w x 22"d x 28"h
1949
An extremely rare item that is Heywood-Wakefield's most imaginative design, combining the unconventional use of tambour doors placed on different levels, an asymmetrically shaped top, and long tapered legs on one end. It resembles no other piece made by the company.
$1200-1400

M546 Detail
The tambour doors open to reveal two compartments fitted with a shelf. Could be used as a desk or as a vanity with an optional mirror.

Kohinoor Bed
M140
Available in twin or full sizes
1949–1951
The sharpness of Kohinoor is reiterated in the design of the bed. The headboard and footboard have a downward swag across the length and outward flare on the sides. Notice the concave molding across the footboard. It makes a stronger statement than most Heywood-Wakefield beds.
$200-300

M546 Detail
The asymmetrical top is 22" deep on the right side and 16" deep on the left, which also rises to 35" high. Notice how the tambour door completely turns the right corner of the desk.

**Kohinoor Nightstand
M148**
20"w x 16"d x 24"h
1949–1951
The long legs are appealing, although it is less functional than the Encore nightstand.
$150-200

**Sculptura 4-Drawer Chest
M772**
38"w x 19"d x 39"h
1952–1959
A junior-sized highboy. All of Sculptura dressers and chests have drawers at the same level so that two or more units placed next to one another create a uniform "wall of drawers."
$350-550

**Sculptura 5-Drawer Chest
M792**
38"w x 19"d x 48"h
1953–1959
The year after Kohinoor was discontinued, the Sculptura group was introduced. The main style feature was a three-section drawer front with a wavy centerpiece that, like Kohinoor's drawers, functioned as a handle. Unique to Sculptura bedroom pieces were the finished drawer dividers exposed on the front of the case, and drawers that were recessed. It included two more dresser options than Kohinoor and ran for eight years, second only to Encore. The M792 was Heywood-Wakefield's tallest and widest highboy.
$450-650

Sculptura Triple Dresser
M779
62"w x 19"d x 31"h
1952–1959
A great-looking, functional item with six large outer drawers and three wavy lingerie drawers down the center. Trumped for drawer space only by the Encore triple dresser.
$700-900

Sculptura Triple Dresser with Mirror
M779-575
62"w x 19"d x 31"h
Mirror : M575
50"w x 34"h
1952–1959
$800-1000

**Sculptura Mr. and Mrs. Dresser
M774**
56"w x 19"d x 31"h
1952–1959
This dresser, like its Encore counterpart, was available with the large M575 mirror or the smaller, tilting M525 mirror.
$500-700

**Sculptura 3-Drawer Dresser with Mirror
M771**
46"w x 19"d x 31"h
Mirror: M573
32"w x 34"h
1952–1956
Not obvious is the slightly bowed front top on all Sculptura dressers and chests which compensated for the extra dimension created by the wavy drawer centers.
$300-500

Sculptura Dresser with 2-Door Deck Top
M781 on M771
42"w x 16"d x 19"h deck top
46"w x 19"d x 50"h over all
1952–1953
An extremely rare item •composed of a two door cabinet placed on a three-drawer dresser.
$650-850

Sculptura Vanity Stool
M777
20"diam. x 16"h
1952–1959
The X-base on this revolving stool is the same design found on the large, square M392G coffee table, designed two years earlier.
$150-200

M781 on M771 Detail
The doors, which also have the molded wave design, open to reveal a shelved compartment.

Sculptura Nightstand
M778
20"w x 16"d x 24"h
1952–1959
This has the same X-base as the M777. The drawer is opened by a finger recess on the bottom edge.
$200-250

M776 Detail
Notice how the wavy handle portion of the drawer front is joined to the steam bent outer panel in keeping with the curved section of the vanity's base.

Sculptura Vanity and Stool
M776 with M777
50"w x 18"d x 20"h
62" over all height
1952–1959
Although not produced in large numbers, the asymmetrical Sculptura vanity is every bit as stylish as the Kohinoor vanity and has a full-length mirror.
$400-600

Sculptura Bed
M770
Available in twin or full sizes
1952–1959
This simple design is united with the rest of the suite by its wavy molding across the footboard.
$200-300

M770 with M778 night stands
The Sculptura pieces make a guest bed room cheerful and inviting.

Cabinet Utility Headboard
M780
82"w x 11"d x 32.5"h
1952–1955
Available only in full size. Was sold with either Encore or Sculptura.
$400-600

M780 Detail
The doors drop open to provide a handy shelf.

King-sized Utility Headboard
M790 6/6
81"w x 11"d x 37"h
1953-1954
One of Heywood-Wakefield's only king-sized beds, it was originally offered as a way to push two twin beds together. Open and closed compartments preclude the need for bedside tables. There's enough depth on top for a lamp. The sliding center doors are inserted at an interesting slant.
$400-600

Utility Headboard
M1520
Available in twin, full, and king sizes
1956–1966
A very basic cabinet headboard offered in three sizes.
$100-200

**Cadence Utility Headboard
M1110**
Available in full or king sizes
84"w x 14.5"d x 32"h full size
1955–1957
From the Cadence group which, although part of the Heywood-Wakefield Modern line, was largely a failed design experiment. Metal knobs and overhanging tops on all of the bedroom pieces were a misguided departure from the classic Heywood-Wakefield style. The utility bed, shown here modified after-market to make it queen-sized, has design merit for its cantilevered night table ends and use of tambour doors.
$400-600

M1110 4/6 Detail
An overview shows the interesting shape of the cabinet ends of the bed. This daring style was absent in the other Cadence pieces.

4. Dining Rooms

Heywood-Wakefield dining rooms offered a great range of possibilities. At any given time several chair styles were available with several table styles, giving consumers options when furnishing their houses. The same was true for dining room case pieces. All servers, buffets, and credenzas were sold with or without china closet tops and sometimes there were different tops to choose from. As time went on the overall trend seemed to be that the choices and flexibility of building a dining room set increased. Several pieces had longer production runs in the 1950s, which enabled a buyer, for example, to add chairs to a dining room set years after the original purchase. The M154 chair was made from 1950 until the modern era ended in 1966 with only a slight change. Its long run can be credited to its success as a style and its corresponding popularity. The M555, another design standout, lasted from 1950 to 1959.

Flexibility within dining room sets was largely achieved with extension and drop leaf tables. Although all Heywood-Wakefield's dining tables were built to expand for different situations, it was their ten different drop leaf styles that allowed the user the most choices. In fact, many drop leaf tables were also extension tables sold with two leaves. Various looks and functional settings could be achieved with the M197 drop leaf table. It was a true chameleon, changing from a 26" breakfast table for two to a 94" banquet table for ten. In terms of style, there was an enormous difference between the C2932G and the M197 tables. The first had a strong 1930s streamlined modern look accentuated by bent wood stretchers connecting the legs to the center pedestals. The other had an extremely biomorphic design created by tapering, spidery boomerang legs. The same style evolution is illustrated by comparing a C2794 chair with bent wood legs and swooping one-piece backrest and seat with an M154 "dog bone" chair with its free form opening in the back. They are vastly different.

If there is one constant in the chair designs, it is that none are so overly concerned with style that comfort became an afterthought. None make the user feel he's sitting on a sculpture. This practicality was and is a major contributing factor to Heywood Wakefield's popularity.

Dining room case pieces evolved in a similar way to bedroom case pieces. Earlier servers and buffets were more rounded in the front than later ones. Doors and drawers were steam-bent to achieve this look. Many of the 1950s pieces achieved the more biomorphic look primarily with the introduction of a shapely, organic handle on the doors and Encore handles on the drawers. Another parallel to bedroom sets worth noting among dining room pieces was the introduction of more sizes and choices by the 1950s. Large china closet tops were available to sit on the longer bases. Only smaller china closets were produced during the prewar and war period. The M176 corner cupboard was similarly enlarged from the earlier C3348. In 1956, the M1542 buffet was introduced, unique not only for its tambour door, but for its asymmetrical design. (Asymmetry was a post-war trait seen on only a few case items, including Kohinoor, Sculptura and Encore vanities.) Heywood-Wakefield kept in tune with the post-war demand for more choices, including larger, more functional items.

From the 1940 catalog.

From a 1950 promotional mailer.

Chairs

Dimensions include width of seat and overall height.

Upholstery tacks along side of chair are original.

C2794C
19"w x 33"h
1936–1941
Designer: Gilbert Rohde
The classic 1930's streamlined look. Back legs are solid bent maple, not laminated. Resembles designs Rohde created for other manufacturers.
$150-200

C2794A
15.5"w x 33"h
1936–1941
Designer: Gilbert Rohde
This side chair is narrower than the more generously proportioned armchair.
$100-150

C3535A
16"w x 35"h
1939-1943
$75-125

C2794A

C3595C
18"w x 34"h
1940–1944
$75-125

C3526A
15.5"w x 33"h
1939–1940
Designer: Gilbert Rohde
An open wood frame version of the C2794A design.
$100-150

C3526A

M157C
18"w x 34"h
1947–1950
This has the original chartreuse vinyl–a popular choice in the late 1940s.
$75-125

M155A
18"w x 33"h
1947–1950
A very simple, sturdy design that is timeless.
$75-125

M157A
18"w x 34"h
1947-1950
The pink poinsettia fabric is original, and very representative of the era.
$50-100

M152A
17"w x 34"h
1947–1950
$40-80

M555C
21"w x 34"h
1950–1955
Heywood-Wakefield's most elegant chair design after 1950. The oversized armchair is unique in that its front leg extends up to its arm.
$150-200

Opposite page
Left: **M154C**
18"w x 34"h
1950–1955
Heywood-Wakefield's best chair, known as the dog bone chair, perfectly captures the optimistic feeling of the 1950's. An excellent example of biomorphism and perhaps their single best item.
$150-200

Right: **M154A**
18"w x 33"h
1950–1955
$100-150

M555A
18"w x 32.5"h
1950–1955
The side chair is shorter and narrower than the armchair.
$100-150

M555A Detail
Notice the thin sculpted edge of the back. The undulating curves resemble a manta ray.

M553C
18"w x 32"h
1950–1953
An example of a less-expensive entry-level style. Heywood-Wakefield produced items in several different price ranges.
$50-100

M553A
17"w x 32"h
1950–1953
$40-80

M151A
17"w x 32"h
1950–1953
The back of this chair resembles a cat's eye.
$50-100

M556C
18"w x 31"h
1952–1954
$75-125

M556C Detail
S-shaped rear leg was crafted from a thicker than usual piece of wood. An extremely sensuous design.
1952–1954

M551A
17"w x 32"h
1952–1955
$40-80

M549C
20"w x 30"h
1953–1966
A modern version of the classic captain's chair
$100-150

M552A
18"w x 32"h
1953–1955
A whimsical trapezoid makes a fun chair back.
$50-100

M554C
18"w x 33"h
1953–1955
This armchair looks ready to blast off!
$75-125

M953C
18"w x 32"h
1954–1955
This chair's back resembles a bow tie.
$75-125

M953A
17"w x 32"h
1954–1955
$50-100

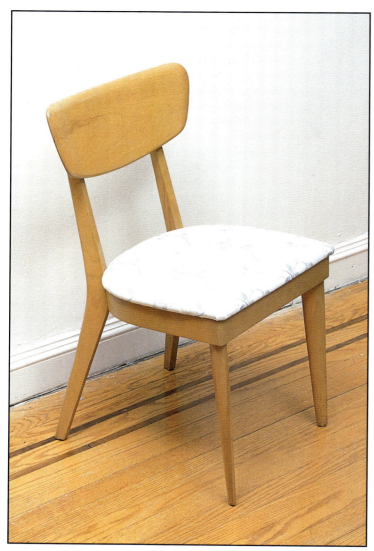

M1551A
18"w x 31.5"h
1956–1966
$40-80

M1552A
19"w x 32"h
1956
Unfortunately, this sensuous design was only produced for one year.
$75-125

M1552C
19"w x 32"h
1956
Notice how the arm curves in three places.
$100-150

M1552C
Detail
The arm makes a 90 degree turn before connecting to the rear leg.

M1553C
20"w x 32.5"h
1956–1966
$75-125

M1553A
18"w x 32.5"h
1956–1966
Another cat's eye chair
$50-100

Tables

Note: all dining tables are the standard 29" high.

Large Extension Table
C2932G
60" x 42"
Opens to 84" x 42" with two 12" leaves
1936–1939
The bent wood stretchers convey the feeling of sweeping motion–a motif of the streamlined era–and add rigidity to this generous-sized table.
$600-800

C2932G with C2794A chairs

C2932G with C2794A chairs
Two center panels on the table base move apart as leaves are inserted.

**Small Extension Table
C3955G**
40" x 30"
10" leaf
1941–1942
A very basic model designed for small spaces and small budgets.
$200-300

**Large Extension Table
C3347G**
54" x 36"
Opens to 78" x 36" with two 12" leaves
1938–1939
A similar design to the C2932G but in a more intimate size.
$350-450

**5-leg Extension Table
M165G**
60" x 42"
Opens to 90" x 42" with two 15" leaves
1947–1952
This post-war table shows a shift from the 1930s streamlined look to a more timeless design. The center leg adds stability when the leaves are used.
$500-700

M165G with M155 chairs.
Plenty of elbow room for six people

M165G with M155 chairs
Can accommodate ten people

M165G with M155 chairs

M169G with M552 chairs

Junior Extension Table
M169G
50" x 34"
Opens to 64" x 34" with one 14" leaf
1950–1955
A very popular table with severely rounded corners—as oval as a rectangle can be.
$350-450

M169G with M552 chairs
Comfortable seating for six

5-leg Extension Table
M789G
60" x 42"
Opens to 90" x 42" with two 15" leaves
1953–1955
This five-leg table with arched legs has a more biomorphic look than the M165G.
$500-700

M789G with M555 chairs
Can accommodate ten when fully extended

Junior Extension Table
M189G
54" x 36"
Opens to 72" x 36" with one 18" leaf
1951–1955
The shaped apron and grooved legs make this a unique design.
$400-500

M189G with M154 chairs

M189G with M154 chairs
Comfortable seating for six with room for two more if necessary

Junior Extension Table
M1558G
54" x 38"
Opens to 72" x 38" with one 18" leaf
1956–1966
A sharper edge on the top that overhangs the apron, and slimmer legs are both representative of the late 1950s design shift.
$350-450

M1558G with M154 Chairs
The M154 chair was redesigned as the M1554 in 1956, with slimmer front legs to match this table.

Round Extension Table
M950G
48" diameter
Opens to a 62" x 48" oval with one 14" leaf
1954–1955
The arched legs and soft apron give this simple, round table its appealing style.
$450-650

M950G
Seating for six when extended.

Bottom left: **Round Extension Table with M154 Chairs M1568G**
48" diameter
Opens to a 72" x 48" oval with two 12" leaves
1958–1959
The sharp-edged top, recessed apron and straight legs were late 1950s style trends.
$450-650

Bottom right: **M1568G with M154 Chairs**
Insert two leaves to make a great conference table.

Triple Pedestal Drop Leaf Extension Table
M197G
26" x 40" closed
Two 18" leaves
1948–1955
Heywood-Wakefield's top-of-the-line table and their longest table when fully opened. Its three boomerang legs and wing-supported drop leaves make it an unparalleled example of 1950s design.
$700-900

M197G
42" x 40"
Can be used against a wall with one leaf dropped.

M197G
58" x 40"
The raised leaves reveal an extremely animated design.

M197G
26" x 40" closed
The ultimate in flexibility—a table for every occasion. Redesigned in 1956 as the M1597G with sharper edges and slimmer legs, this same basic design was produced from 1948 to 1966, the longest run of any Heywood-Wakefield dining table.

M197G
42" x 40"

M197G
58" x 40"

M197G
94" x 40" with two leaves inserted
Comfortable seating for ten people

M197G
76" x 40" with one leaf inserted

M197G Detail
The support for the center pedestal spans the telescopic tracks that enable the large expansion. The pedestal automatically finds the center when the table is fully open.

M197G table with M154 Chairs
The classic table and chair combination. Also shown: the M328W, which can be used as a server and liquor cabinet.

Double Pedestal Drop Leaf Extension Table
M786G
22" x 38"
Two 12" leaves
1952–1955
A smaller relative of the M197G with the same flexibility. Its semi-circular drop leaves appeal to those who want an oval table.
$450-650

Top right: **M786G**
38" x 38"

Bottom right: **M786G**
54" x 38"

M786G
54" x 38"

M786G
66" x 38" with one leaf

M786G
78" x 38" with two leaves
Comfortably seats eight

Harmonic Drop Leaf Extension Table
M989G
26" x 42"
Two 10" leaves
1954–1955
A sharper-edged top with more pointed corners—the beginnings of a late 1950s look.
$350-450

M989G
62" x 42"

M989G
44" x 42"

M989G
72" x 42" with one leaf
82" x 42" when fully open

Double Pedestal Drop Leaf Extension Table
M1556G
22" x 38"
Two 12" leaves
1956–1961
Another smaller relative of the M197G, this time with rectangular drop leaves.
$450-650

M1556G
54" x 38"

M1556G
78" x 38" with two leaves

M1556G
38" x 38"

**Gate-leg Drop Leaf Table
M166G**
14" x 36" closed
1947–1955
Two hinged legs swing out on each end to support large drop leaves. Heywood-Wakefield's smallest table, when closed, can be used as a console in a small room or hallway.
$350-450

M166G
37" x 36" half open

M166G
60" x 36" open

M166G with M552 Chairs
Makes a charming breakfast table in this setting

M166G
14" x 36" closed
Takes up very little space when closed

M166G
60" x 36" open
Two legs remain in the center for stability while the rudder-like legs swing out on each side—a very animated design.

Drop Leaf Service Cart
M394G
20"x 38"
1951–1952
A hard to find item, it's useful for serving cocktails or dessert.
$450-650

M394G
34"x 38" with one leaf up

M394G
48"x 38" fully open
It appears as if it wants to fly.

M394G and M155 Chairs
Makes an excellent breakfast table for an eat-in kitchen

Dining Room Case Pieces

Airflow Buffet
C3318
52"w x 19"d x 34"h
1937–1939
Designer: Leo Jiranek
The curved-front and centered handles are prime examples of 1930s design. The vertical ridges are handles on the doors and, by design, appear connected to the handles on the full-length bottom drawer.
$400-600

Buffet
C3709
48"l x 18"d x 35"h
1940–1942
A hard-to-find item that is desirable perhaps for the unique way it sits high off the floor on tall legs– uncharacteristic of Heywood-Wakefield case furniture.
$500-700

Left: **Airflow China Closet C3316 on C3317**
29"w x 12"d x 34"h top
32"w x 18"d x 30"h base
64" over all height
1937–1939
Designer: Leo Jiranek
The Airflow china and buffet are hard to find due to their age.
$400-600

Right: **C3316 on C3317** Detail
The large door that swings open is an unusual feature on Heywood-Wakefield china closets—most had sliding glass doors. The base also has a large, swinging door.

China Top on Server
M175 on M590
32"w x 14.5"d x 32"h top
64" high over all
1950–1955
One of Heywood-Wakefield's most heavily produced items, it allows the display of china while occupying only 34" of horizontal floor space.
$350-450

Server
M590
34"w x 17"d x 32.5"h
1950–1955
Commonly sold as part of many dining room sets; this server has whimsical, free form handles, one of many features that gave Heywood-Wakefield its fun, informal look.
$200-300

M590 Detail
A large interior compartment with a shelf offers lots of storage space.

Buffet
M592
48"w x 18"d x 32.5"h
1950–1955
Like the M590 server, this was a common component of many dining room sets.
$250-350

Credenza
M593
54"w x 18"d x 34"h
1950–1955
A generously sized unit with a full-length top drawer.
$400-600

Buffet with China Top
M999 on M592
46"w x 14"d x 26"h top
58.5" over all height
1954–1955
The slanted china top adds drama to the M592 base. A narrower china top (M375) with the same angled profile was available to sit on the smaller M590 base.
$400-600

Large China Top on Credenza
M198 on M593
52"w x 14"d x 38"h top
72" high over all
1950–1955
The ultimate in storage and display, the M593 base could accommodate three differently configured large china closet tops. The M198 had three independent sliding glass doors to access its compartments.
$700-900

Corner Cabinet
C3348
24"w x 14.5"d x 65"h
1938–1939
This was the first of three corner cabinets produced. The second featured round knobs on the doors and the third, the largest, had cutout handles.
$450-650

Corner Cabinet
M176
28"w x 16"d x 68"h
1948–1955
A difficult piece to find considering its seven year production. Its curved front adds drama to a corner. It has plate grooves on the shelves to display china.
$600-800

M176
The doors swing open to reveal an adjustable shelf.

M196W Detail
The center drawer slides out and its hinged façade drops to create a handy secretary desk. Notice that the full length bottom drawer is styled so that on first sight it doesn't look like a drawer.

Credenza with Desk Drawer
M196W
54"l x 18"d x 34"h
1950
Designer: Joseph Carr
This rare and stylish unit features four concave doors, a full-length concave drawer along the bottom, and three concave drawers along the top, the center one being a hidden desk. Produced for only one year–possibly in an attempt to make dining room pieces that paralleled the Kohinoor bedroom style. It was also available in a two door 36" wide server and a three door 48" buffet.
$550-750

M196W Detail
The attention to detail is incredible here even down to the desk organizer that's scalloped to resemble the concave door façade of the entire credenza.

M196W Detail
Four steam bent concave doors open to reveal more open cabinet space than in most Heywood-Wakefield credenzas.

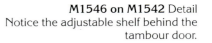
M1546 on M1542 Detail
Notice the adjustable shelf behind the tambour door.

Tambour Door Buffet with China Top
M1546 on M1542
45.5" w x 14" d x 26" h top
50"w x 18"d x 32"h base
58" over all height
A graceful, asymmetrical design. The china top has sliding glass doors.
$500-700

Crown Glass China Closet on Credenza
M1547 on M1543
56"w x 15"d x 35"h top
67" over all height
1956–1965
A great, hard-to-find item with plenty of functional space. Three swing open doors have large, unusual, curved glass panels.
$800-1000

Credenza
M1543
60"w x 18"d x 32"h
1956–1965
The framed panel doors and spiked legs are late 1950s features. Also, the 60" length is unprecedented in Heywood-Wakefield dining room pieces produced earlier.

Server
M1597
36"w x 17"d x 30"h
1961–1966
A perfect companion to the M1543 credenza.
$200-300

Crown Glass China Closet on Credenza
M1547 on M1544
M1544–60"w x 18"d x 32"h
1956–1965
The M1544 was an alternative to the M1543 as a base for the three-door crown glass china cabinet. Both pieces had a felt-lined drawer for silverware.
$800-1000

5. Living Rooms

Upholstered sofas and chairs are among the hardest pieces to find. It is unclear whether fewer of these pieces were originally produced than bedroom or dining room pieces, or if more of them were disposed of over the years as they became worn. Perhaps both are factors. The Aristocraft seating line, which featured three designs of open-arm, exposed-wood framed seating, with loose back and bottom cushions, is the most readily available upholstered furniture. Immensely popular because of the amount of visible wood, the line was a blessing for Heywood-Wakefield allowing the factories to utilize smaller scraps of wood that may otherwise have been wasted. The CM-929-66 sofa alone consists of 34 mostly small pieces assembled into a unified and graceful sofa frame. Aside from visual lightness, Aristocraft seating was physically light which allowed easy rearranging.

Fully upholstered sofas and chairs were frequently just as stylish even though their curvy frames were covered by upholstery. Many had wood trim on the fronts and sides of arms to accentuate the lines. Like Aristocraft, they were available in chairs, loveseats, sofas and sectional components.

All one has to do is lift a Heywood-Wakefield sofa to understand the integrity of its construction. Consisting of entirely hardwood frames and steel coil springs, not to mention spring-filled loose cushions, they are superbly put together and very comfortable.

> "The frames of all Heywood-Wakefield upholstered pieces are made from kiln dried, seasoned hardwoods. All frames are rigidly screwed, glued, and corner blocked. Only solid Birch wood is used in the exposed elements on Heywood-Wakefield upholstered furniture." From the 1951 catalog.

Of course, a good seating group is complemented by the tables that surround it. Heywood-Wakefield produced a full line of living room tables that harmonize with their seating. They made coffee tables of varying lengths and shapes as well as end tables and occasional tables in an assortment of shapes and configurations. These pieces completed the look of Heywood-Wakefield's living room groups. Some of the most popular items were the various step end tables, which are now among the most abundant living room pieces available. Another popular item was the corner table that allowed the user to arrange Heywood-Wakefield's sectional seating in interesting ways. L-shaped seating arrangements were heavily promoted in company sales literature as a way to create atmosphere and divide living room spaces at a time when new home construction often eliminated formal dining rooms.

Ultimately, with the use of some imagination, one can now find uses for certain items that were never intended by the company. A case in point is the M364G end table which, although produced as a lamp table makes an excellent TV/VCR stand. Many occasional tables also work as bedside tables and vice versa. Several upholstered chairs are the right size to put in a bedroom corner or beside a desk.

Seating

Note: All seating dimensions are as follows: Width is measured between arms (i.e. usable seating space). Depth and height are overall dimensions.

Aristocraft Sectional Sofa
CM367, CM367LC, CM367RC
Each section is 22"w x 34"d x 32"h
1950–1953
Can be used as seen here or as an L-shaped arrangement. More armless fillers can be added. Also available as a full-length davenport or loveseat.
$500-700

CM367, CM367LC, CM367RC
Shown here without cushions to display the slats that are normally visible from the back, woodwork that made Aristocraft seating unmistakably Heywood-Wakefield. Removable cushions were easy and cost-effective to reupholster.

CM 367C
Without cushions one can fully appreciate the extremely bent arms that are a hallmark of Heywood-Wakefield design.

Aristocraft Arm Chair
CM 367C
22"w x 34"d x 32"h
1950–1953
A very inviting arm chair.
$350-450

Aristocraft Double Filler
CM368LC
44"w x 34"d x 32"h
1952–1953
Introduced two years into the production run, the double fillers are rather uncommon. They were also available with one 44" cushion across the back and one across the seat.
$300-400

Aristocraft Platform Rocker
CM367D
22"w x 34"d x 37"h
1952–1953
Extremely rare and very comfortable as it rocks quietly on springs. Notice the back is higher than the CM367C chair. A higher back is also available in the CM367R stationary chair.
$500-700

CM367D
Shown with an M517 vanity stool used as an ottoman.

Aristocraft Davenport
CM389–68
68" x 36" x 35"
1951–1953
Another of the three basic Aristocraft styles, the spring-filled cushions are noticeably thicker than those on the M367 Aristocraft series. The slatted arms lend visual and structural substance.
$800-1000

Aristocraft Sectional Sofa
CM388, CM388LC, CM388RC
23"w x 36"d x 35"h each section
1951–1953
A cozy three-piece arrangement with an M338G corner table
$600-800

**Aristocraft Arm Chair
CM388C**
23"w x 36"d x 35"h
1951–1953
The closest thing to a Stickley Morris chair built after World War II. Original floral upholstery fabric.
$400-500

CM388C
It has an almost aeronautical look when seen from the back.

Aristocraft Davenport
CM929-66
66"w x 36"d x 31"h
1954–1966
The third of three Aristocraft styles, it had a sleek lower back and bent wood arms, reminiscent of well-known Danish Modern arm styles of the 1950s. Original cosmic upholstery fabric.
$800-1000

CM929-66
Plenty of woodwork to admire.

CM929-66
Sleek profile makes it look ready to blast off. The angled back legs resembled tail fins on 1950s cars and, by design, extended slightly further to the rear than the sofa back, preventing the wall from being rubbed.

CM929–66 davenport and **CM927C** chair shown in a consultation group with **M1505** cocktail table and **M993G** lamp table.
Lamp Table
M993G
22"w x 20"d x 25"h
1954–1955

**Aristocraft Arm Chair
CM927C**
23"w x 36"d x 31"h
1954–1966
A pair of CM927C armchairs nicely flanks a M794G step end table. Also shown: M166 table and M152 chairs.
$350-450

Above: Sectional Sofa
C3341RC and C3341LC
22"w x 36"d x 34"h
1937–1938
An early design with an Art Deco influence. Maple panel ends accentuate the handsome profile. Armless fillers were also available.
$400-600

Top right: Sectional Sofa
C3341RC and C3341LC

From the 1937 catalog.
Pictured:
C3341 Sectional Sofa
C3327G Corner Table
C2927G End Table

Davenport
C3367-66
66"w x 35"d x 32"h
1938–1939
Designer: Alfons Bach
A superb early design with Art Deco styling accentuated by the side panels and wood trim on the arms.
$800-1000

Davenport and Armchair
C3980–68 and C3980C
68"w x 36"d x 32"h
23"w x 36"d x 32"h
1941–1944
An excellent compromise—fully upholstered frames with exposed arms and legs to show some wood. Also shown: M322 bookcase.
Davenport, 800-1000; chair, $300-400

Davenport
C3987–66
66"w x 36"d x 32"h
1941–1944
Designer: Joseph Carr
A very warm and inviting sofa.
$800-1000

C3987–66
Notice the articulated arm seen in profile. The bent wood applied to the arm adds the signature Heywood-Wakefield style to the sofa.

Arm Chair
C3985C
22"w x 36"d x 32"h
1941–1944
Designer: Joseph Carr
Matching chair with original fabric sports a factory option–a channeled back.
$300-400

Sectional Sofa
M360LC, M360RC, M363

Right and left arm sections flank three rare, curved M363 fillers to create a fantastic sectional sofa. Also shown: M538 Encore night stands used as end tables and M312G nesting tables.
$900-1100

M360RC Detail
A simple wood teardrop makes this sofa more stylish than one with a plain fabric arm.

Davenport
M358-68
68"l x 36"d x 32"h
1950–1953
A great angular zigzag arm gave this sofa an atomic profile.
$800-1000

Arm Chair
M355C
22"l x 36"w x 32"h
1950–1953
The original swirl patterned fabric provides a perfect contrast to the angular lines of the chair.
$300-400

Arm Chair
M560C
23"w x 36"d x 32"h
1951–1953
The arms of this chair resembled automobile fenders. Notice the splayed legs on this and later 1950s upholstered pieces.
$350-450

Arm Chair
M595C
26"w x 36"d x 30"h
1954–1955
Armchair matches the M596 sofa, shown here reupholstered in 1950s abstract patterned fabric.
$300-400

Sectional Sofa
M596RC, M596LC
50"w x 36"d x 30"h each section
1954–1955
An office lounge area is created by a pair of double fillers that resemble "bench style" automotive seats. The seat cushions are not removable, creating a very clean design. Also shown: M322 bookcase, M392 cocktail table, M992G end tables.
M992G end table
28"w x 16" d x 21"h
1954–1955
$700-900

M595C Detail
A side view providaes a glimpse of the unusually angled arms.

Barrel Chair
C3326C
22"w x 30"d x 34"h
1937–1939
An Art Deco-influenced chair looks as if it was originally intended for furnishing an office.
$150-200

Arm Chair
M1170C
25"w x 35"d x 30"h
1955–1957
$250-350

Occasional Chair
C3325C
20"d x 18.5"w x 35"h
1937–1940
An elegant early design featuring steam bent arms.
$250-350

Pull-up Chair
M340C
22"w x 32"d x 33"h
1949–1952
Lightweight, movable seating that can be used in a small space or a bedroom.
$150-200

M340C

Tub Chair
M345C
24"w x 18"d x 33"h
1950–1957

An animated, curvaceous style which adds an informal feel to spaces that require a comfortable, but smaller scaled lounge chair. Also shown: M306G cocktail table and C3549G lamp table. (Sofa is not Heywood-Wakefield)
$150-250

**Open-arm Tub Chair
M568C**
23"w x 32"d x 30"h
1951–1958
An inventive design with arms that resemble elephant tusks.
$200-275

M568C Detail

**Pull-up Chair
M569C**
23"w x 32"d x 32.5"h
1951–1959
A good chair for those who prefer angular over rounded lines.
$150-250

Occasional Tables

Cocktail Table with Drawer
C3717G
1940–1942
37"l x 17"w x 16"h
From the 1940 catalog.
$275-375

Top right: **Round Cocktail Table**
M306G
32"diam. x 16"h
1947–1955
An extremely popular cocktail table. Redesigned slightly in 1956 as the M1576, the basic design was in production from 1947 to 1961. Has the Heywood-Wakefield signature spider legs and a handy revolving top.
$200-300

Right: **M306G** Detail
Notice how the legs are mounted to an independent platform that covers the ball bearing swivel. The two horizontal wood strips are anti-warping cleats applied to ensure that the 32" top maintains its integrity.

Cocktail Table
M319G
40"l x 22"w x 16"h
1949–1954
This table has sculpted guardrails to prevent cocktails from falling over the edge.
$200-300

Square Cocktail Table
M307G
36" square x 16"h
1949–1952
One of the hardest-to-find cocktail tables. The size of the top and the span of the legs are impressive.
$300-400

M307G
The gradually tapered top is more interesting than an exact square.

Cocktail Table
M316G
36"l x 19"w x 16"h
1949
Produced for only one year, this functional table was probably overshadowed by Heywood-Wakefield's more curvaceous designs.
$200-300

Cocktail Table
M335
36"l x 19"w x 16"h
1950–1953
Heywood-Wakefield's best-conceived cocktail table. Small enough to fit any living area, its lower shelf makes it even more functional than the larger M319G table. Like most of their rectangular tables, the sides are gradually tapered.
$225-325

Square Cocktail Table
M392G
36" square x 16"h
1950–1955
Another oversized square table with a notable difference from the M307G. The sides taper in the opposite direction.
$300-400

M392G Detail
Notice how the legs are anchored to the underside of the top.

**Large Cocktail Table
M795G**
50"l x 22"w x 16"h
1953–1955
One of the largest and most appealing cocktail tables built, with arched legs emerging from an unusual pointed apron. Has the definitive 1950s flair.
$300-400

**Cocktail Table
M991G**
36"l x 19"w x 16"h
1954–1955
Introduced one year after the larger M795G, this table's added shelf compensated for its smaller overall size.
$200-300

Cocktail Table with Drawer
M905G
40"l x 20"w x 16"h
1954–1955
A very rare table designed with a bonus–hidden storage. This rectangular table, in contrast to most others, has straight sides and tapered ends.
$400-500

M905G
A full-length drawer opens from underneath with a recessed finger grip.

Cocktail Table
M1505
52"l x 20"w x 15"h
1957–1966
One of Heywood-Wakefield's longest cocktail tables, it stands up to a long sofa. Its thin edge and sharp legs indicate its late production.
$300-400

**3-Tier End Table
C3170G**
27"l x 14"w x 21"h
1936–1939
The first of many step end tables produced by Heywood-Wakefield. It is almost constructivist in its simplicity.
$100-200

C3753G
Bottom shelf has built-in bookends.

**3-Tier End Table
C3753G**
30"l x 15"w x 22"h
1940–1944
A design similar to the C3170G with the more recognizable Heywood-Wakefield curves.
$150-250

**3-Tier End Table
M304G**
30"l x 15"w x 22"h
1947–1949
Another fine three-tier table with a leggier design.
$150-250

**Step End Table
M308G**
30"l x 17"w x 22"h
1948–1953
One of the single most heavily
produced items.
$75-150

**Wedge Step End Table
M396G**
30"l x 22"w x 22"h
1950–1953
The wedge shape helps create curved seating arrangements when placed between upholstered fillers.
$100-200

**Step End Table with Drawer
M794G**
30"l x 18"w x 22"h
1953–1955
A step end table fitted with a storage drawer to hide clutter. Also shown; CM927C arm chairs.
$175-275

**Step End Table
M908G**
30"l x 16"w x 22"h
1954–1955
$100-200

**Round Lamp Table
C3549G**
22" diam. x 26"h
1939–1940
A very simple but pleasing design.
$175-275

**Step End Table
M1584G**
30"l x 20"w 22.5"h
1956–1957
The horizontal stretchers between the front and rear legs were similar to those on popular Danish Modern tables of the same era.
$100-200

**Lamp Table
M337G**
21"l x 21"w x 25"h
1950–1953
The 25" height is useful in places where the standard 22" end table is too short. Can be used as a bedside table.
$150-250

M364G
Its generously sized top makes a perfect television stand, and its lower tier is ideal for a VCR.

**Lamp Table
M364G**
26"l x 24"w x 26"h
1950–1955
A great space age design. The angular flare of the sides is very characteristic of the 1950s.
$225-325

Center Table
M393G
30"x 26"h
1950–1952
A very rare item, it looks like a modern version of the traditional mahogany occasional table.
$300-400

2-Tier End Table
C2927G
26"l x 11"w x 21"h
1936–1938
An early table which looks almost too straight to be Heywood-Wakefield.
$100-200

End Table
C3962G
28"w x 15"w x 21"h
1941–1942
An attractive oval two-tier table supported by steam bent sides. One of only two oval end table styles produced by Heywood-Wakefield.
$150-250

C3962G Detail
A side view shows the unusual floating effect of the top.

**2-Tier End Table
M391G**
28"l x 16"w x 22"h
1950–1952
Perfect for a small television and VCR.
$150-250

**Magazine Rack End Table
M503G**
28"l x 15"w 22"h
1953–1957
A unique, upright magazine rack temptingly displays periodicals to potential readers.
$175-275

**2-Tier End Table
M791G**
28"l x 16"w x 21"h
1952–1953
Observe that the classic, arched legs match those on the M337G lamp table, the M335G cocktail table, and the M308 step end table. Several Heywood-Wakefield living room tables were styled in groups to harmonize with each other.
$125-225

**2-Tier Corner Table
CM970G**
30"L x 30"W x 23"H
1954–1955
$100-200

**2-Tier End Table
M1502G**
30"l x 20"d x 21"h
1957–1966
A later end table that is more generously-sized than the earlier M791G.
$150-250

**2-Tier Corner Table
M338G**
32"l x 32"w x 21"h
1950–1953
This large table was used to build sectional seating arrangements.
$200-300

Nesting Tables
M312G
21"l x 15"w x 24"h–large
19"l x 13.5"w x 23"h–medium
17"l x 12"w x 22"h–small
1949–1953
One of the most pleasing items Heywood-Wakefield produced, these tables are engaging to look at no matter how they are arranged.
$400-600

Left: **Triangular Nesting Tables M902G**
27"l x 19.5"w x 24"h– large
27"l x 19.5"w x 21.75"h–medium
27"l x 19.5"w x 19.5"h–small
1954–1955
Much rarer than the M312G and even more fun to arrange.
$500-700

Center & Right:
M902G

6. Utility Pieces

Some of the best Heywood-Wakefield pieces were the ones not built specifically for the bedroom, living room, or dining room. They were accessory items that rounded out the Modern Line and could take Heywood-Wakefield into the office or workplace. These pieces were desks, shelves, and various storage units. Many of these items are hard to find for the simple reason that while every home had at least one bedroom, a dining room or dining/living areas, not every home had an office or den.

One of Heywood-Wakefield's most successful items was the M320 kneehole desk. With minor design modification, it ran almost the entire 30-year span of their Modern Line. Besides the beauty of its steam-bent drawers, it is extremely functional as the entire case consists of drawers. It also had a fully finished back so that it did not necessarily need to be used against a wall. Many of the shelving units and storage cabinets were designed with a plan. They were the same height so that one could assemble harmonious wall units of pieces that had different uses. Assembling a unit around the M322 bookcase was an excellent way to increase the functionality of a room's corners.

Speaking of function, Heywood-Wakefield's M505 on M504 room divider was one of the cleverest ways to divide a large area. It had a bookshelf or display unit on the top half and a credenza or secretary on the bottom half. Very few, if any, other mid-century furniture companies ever made room dividers, let alone one so useful and attractive. They were produced in small numbers, however, and are consequently hard to find.

DESKS

C3539W with C2794A Chair
The Rohde chair is particularly well suited to this vanity/desk design.

C3539W
The gracefully curved, fully finished back is best appreciated if not placed against a wall.

Crescendo Vanity/Desk
C3539W
48"w x 21"d x 30"h
1939–1940
Designer: Count Alexis de Sakhnoffsky
Heywood-Wakefield's first kneehole desk with steam bent drawers. This same basic design lasted until 1966 with minor design and size changes. It was also available as a vanity with a wall-mounted mirror as part of the Crescendo bedroom set.
$600–800

Kneehole Desk
M320W
50"w x 24"d x 30"h
1950-1965
This was actually the fourth version of Count Sakhnoffsky's original design. The second was the smaller C3978W, which was 46"w x 21"d x 30"h, and the third was the M315W, which was equal in size to the M320W, but had a platform base instead of Encore feet.
$800-1000

Top right: **M320W**
The deep, divided file drawer, cleverly disguised as two drawers, was a useful part of a design which lasted unchanged for 16 years, second only in production length to the M321 bookcase.

Bottom right: **M320W and M155 Chair**
The long top drawer was divided into three sections for organized storage.

Vanity Desk
M926
50"w x 22"d x 29"h
1954–1956
One of Heywood-Wakefield's sexiest designs. Fewer drawers than the M320 desk, but a much leggier design. It is also much harder to find.
$1000-1200

M926 Detail
Like all Heywood-Wakefield desks, the back is fully finished.

M926 and M154 chair
A perfect combination

Student Desk
M783W
44"w x 22"d x 30"h
1952–1961
A useful design that accommodates books on one side. Works great with the drawer end against a wall and the bookshelf end thrust into the room.
$500-700

M783W and M553 Chair
Like the M320 desk, this desk has a deep file drawer and a full-length top drawer.

Table Desk
M327W
40"w x 20"d x 30"h
1950–1954
An uncommon writing desk that can work beside a kneehole desk as a computer table or can be used as a foyer piece.
$350-450

M1575 and M1565 Chair
The chair was designed specifically for use with this desk.

**Princess desk
M1575**
32"w x 24"d x 33.5"h
1964–1965
An extremely rare and elegant item that resembles no other piece produced by Heywood-Wakefield.
$900-1100

M327W Detail
Fitted with a useful pencil drawer.

M1575 Detail
The interior is fitted with sectioned organizers and a recessed pencil drawer.

M1575 Detail
The slim tambour-top profile, the bullet-shaped side, and sharp tapered legs make up one of Heywood-Wakefield's slickest designs.

**Princess desk chair
M1565**
A modern version of a ladder-back chair.
$100-200

M328W and M154 Chair
Useful as a desk, it is fitted with the adjustable organizer shown.

Left: **Desk Bookcase C3977W**
60"l x 12"d x 44"h
1941–1942
A nice symmetrical design with several practical uses. Notice how it differs from the later M328W desk bookcase.
$600-800

Above: **Desk Bookcase M328W**
60"w x 13"d x 42"h
1951–1954
This large, multifunctional item has a nice, asymmetrical design. It serves as a secretary, chest, and adjustable bookcase. Even though it's one of Heywood-Wakefield's largest items, its 13" depth works well in narrow rooms. A great, hard-to-find item.
$700-900

M389W and M154 chair
Contains an adjustable interior organizer.

Desk Chest
M389W
30"w x 13"d x 42"h
1952–1954
Issued one year after the M328W as a smaller unit. Just as hard to find, it is ideal for a narrow, shallow space.
$400-600

Miscellaneous Storage

**Corner Bookcase
M322**
28" from corner to each end x 11"d x 32.5"h
1947–1961
Harder to find than the M321 straight bookcase, the M322 is great to build a modular storage unit around or to use on its own. Holds a surprising number of books.
$300-400

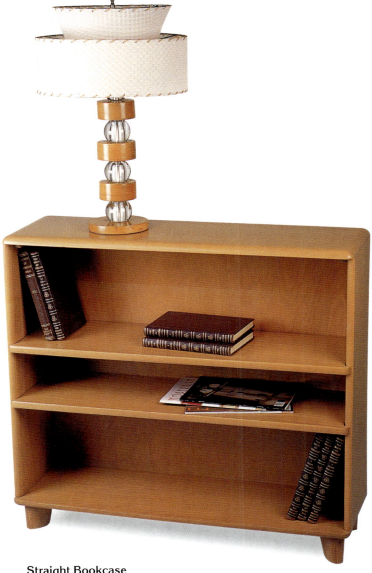

M322 Detail
Notice that the 90 degree back corner is softened by the gracefully turned front corner.

**Straight Bookcase
M321**
36"w x 11"d x 32.5"h
1947–1965
The longest-running single item produced by Heywood-Wakefield. Has two adjustable shelves. Its over all height of 32.5" was intended to align in modular wall arrangements with several other utility items.
$200-300

Crescendo Pier Chests
C3544
16"w x 14"d x 32.5"h
1939–1940
Designer: Count Alexis de Sakhnoffsky
These very rare and useful chests could be aligned with bookshelves or could be used as tall night stands with the Crescendo bedroom set.
$450-550

Cabinet bookcase
M326
36"w x 11"d x 32.5"h
1952–1961
A perfect companion to the M321 bookshelf offering some enclosed storage to complement the open shelving.
$300-400

C3544 with M321 and M322 Bookcases
The pier chests with bookcases make a great modular corner unit.

**Compartment Bookcase
C2929X**
36"w x 11"d x 32.5"h
1937–1938
An early asymmetrical unit that offered auxiliary storage.
$250-350

**Utility Cabinet
M526**
34"l x 15.5"d x 32.5"h
1952–1953
A hard-to-find item that featured fully enclosed cabinet space. Aligns with pier chests, tambour cases and bookcases.
$350-450

M526 Detail
Notice the anti-warping cleats on the inside of the doors to prevent potential cupping caused by extreme humidity variation.

M395 Detail
Interior is fitted with dividers for organized storage of 12" record albums.

Record Cabinet End Table
M395
28"w x 16.5"d x 22"h
1951–1952
This very desirable, hard-to-find item provided useful cabinet space in an end table height piece.
$500-700

Encore Pier Chest
M528
18"w x 15.5"d x 32.5"h
1952–1954
More than a nightstand, but less than a dresser, this hard-to-find chest provides very functional drawer space.
$350-450

M528 and M539-575x
A pair of pier chests flanking the blanket chest makes a great dressing table unit.

Tambour-Front Chest
M178
44.5"w x 20"d x 32.5"h
1947–1948
Great rare item introducing Heywood-Wakefield's first use of tambour doors. The doors were created by cutting grooves into one large panel (not by gluing individual strips to a canvas backing) to ensure harmonious grain patterns.
$600-800

M178 Detail
The doors slide open to access four drawers fitted into an interior metal framework–an unusual construction feature for Heywood-Wakefield

M177 Detail

Tambour-Front Chest
M177
34"w x 17"d x 32.5"h
1947–1948
Same as the M178, but smaller.
$500-700

Tambour Utility Case
M179
24"w x 17"d x 32.5"h
1949–1954
The third tambour utility case that Heywood-Wakefield made was the smallest, but offered open interior space. This item was produced in greater numbers than its predecessors.
$400-600

M179 Detail
The doors open to reveal a compartment with an adjustable shelf.

M179
These cabinets provide hidden space for a small television set, VCR, and stereo components. Good also for books, CDs, or as a liquor cabinet.

**Server
M590**
34"w x 17"d x 32.5"h
1950–1955
A dining room piece that works great as an entertainment unit, it holds a large television set.
$200-300

C2925G Detail
Entire top pivots into position to open.

Pivot-Top Console Table
C2925G
32"w x 16"d x 28"h
1936–1938
Makes a great hall table or "behind the sofa" table.
$300-400

C2925G Detail
Notice the hidden compartment beneath the top.

C2925G
32"w x 32"d x 28"h–open
Makes a small breakfast or card table when flipped open.

Pivot Top Console M313G
32"l x 16"d x 29"h
32"l x 32"d x 29" open
1951–1952
Functions like C2925G pivot top table with a later, more tapered look.
$300-400

Pivot-top console table and chair C2925G and C3526A chair
Shown as a writing table with a C3526A chair.

M313G Detail
Can be used against a wall with the top lifted open to display its graceful lines.

M505 on M504
The reverse side features all open adjustable shelving for books and knick-knacks.

**Room Divider
M505 on M504**
M505 60"w x 11"d x 30"h
M504 60"w x 18"d x 30"h
1953–1956
Comprised of two components, this is one of the largest and perhaps the single best piece of Heywood-Wakefield. Aside from dividing space, it works as a bookshelf, dining room buffet, secretary, or, against a wall, as a wall unit. Built in very limited numbers.
$1600-2000

M505 on M504 Detail
On one side the doors swing open to reveal enclosed storage space. A wooden tray with built-in stops is stored in the base and can be pulled out on either side. This creates a service shelf for entertaining or a secretary for occasional paperwork.

M505 on M504
A great balanced design with prominent splayed feet nicely set in from the ends. An excellent example of multifunctional furniture designed to divide and make the most of combined living room/dining room space.

Price Guide

BEDROOM FURNITURE

Style #	Description	Years	Value	Page
C3330	Airflow Bed	1937–1939	200–300	20
C3331-333	Airflow Dresser with Mirror	1937–1939	350–550	19
C3332	Airflow Chest	1937–1939	400–600	18
C3338	Airflow Nightstand	1937–1939	150–200	20
C3340	Airflow Vanity	1937–1939	400–600	20
C3562	Skyliner Chest	1939–1940	350–550	21
C3568	Skyliner Nightstand	1939–1940	150–200	21
C3739	Blanket Chest	1940–1942	500–700	22
C3791-795	Rio Dresser with Mirror	1943–1944	350–450	28
C3792	Rio Chest	1943–1944	450–550	28
C3798	Rio Nightstand	1943–1944	150–200	29
C3910	Miami Bed	1941–1942	200–300	28
C3911-915	Miami Dresser with Mirror	1941–1942	300–400	25
C3912	Miami Chest	1941–1942	400–500	25
C3916	Miami Vanity	1941–1942	400–500	26
C3917	Miami Vanity Bench	1941–1942	100–150	27
C3918	Miami Nightstand	1941–1942	150–200	27
C3920	Niagara Bed	1941–1942	200–300	24
C3921-923	Niagara Dresser with Mirror	1941–1942	350–550	23
C3922	Niagara Chest	1941–1942	400–600	23
C3926	Niagara Vanity	1941–1942	450–550	24
C3927	Niagara Vanity Seat	1941–1942	150–200	24
C3928	Niagara Nightstand	1941–1942	175–275	24
M140	Kohinoor Bed	1949–1951	200–300	45
M141-145	Kohinoor 3-Drawer Dresser With Mirror	1949–1951	300–500	42
M142	Kohinoor 4-Drawer Chest	1949–1951	400–600	41
M144-525	Kohinoor Mr. and Mrs. Dresser with Mirror	1949–1951	500–700	42
M146	Kohinoor Vanity	1949–1951	450–650	43
M147	Kohinoor Vanity Stool	1949–1951	150–200	44
M148	Kohinoor Nightstand	1949–1951	150–200	46
M149 on M141	Kohinoor Dresser with Deck Top	1949–1951	650–850	43
M182	Riviera Chest	1947–1948	450–550	29
M188	Riviera Nightstand	1947–1948	150-200	29
M510	Encore Bed	1948–1953	200–300	38
M512	Encore 4-Drawer Chest	1948–1950	350–550	30
M518	Encore Nightstand	1948–1955	150–200	36
M521	Encore 4-Drawer Dresser	1948–1955	350–550	33
M522	Encore 5-Drawer Chest	1948–1955	400–600	30
M523	Encore Utility Chest	1948–1954	325–425	35
M524-525	Encore Mr. and Mrs. Dresser with Mirror	1948–1955	500–700	32
M529-575	Encore Triple Dresser With Mirror	1952–1955	700–900	31
M530	Encore Bed	1950–1953	500–700	40
M532	Encore Double Chest	1954–1955	900–1100	33
M536	Encore Vanity	1950–1953	400–600	35
M537	Encore Vanity Bench	1950–1953	175–225	39
M538	Encore Nightstand	1950–1955	200–275	36
M539-575	Encore Blanket Chest with Mirror	1952–1953	600–800	38
M546	Kohinoor Vanity/Desk	1949	1200–1400	44
M587	Encore Vanity Stool	1953	150–200	39
M770	Sculptura Bed	1952–1959	200–300	50
M771-573	Sculptura 3-Drawer Dresser with Mirror	1952–1959	300–500	48
M772	Sculptura 4-Drawer Chest	1952–1959	350–550	46
M774-575	Sculptura Mr. and Mrs. Dresser with Mirror	1952–1959	500–700	48
M776	Sculptura Vanity	1952–1959	400–600	50
M777	Sculptura Vanity Stool	1952–1959	150–200	49
M778	Sculptura Nightstand	1952–1959	200–250	49
M779-575	Sculptura Triple Dresser With Mirror	1952–1959	800–1000	47
M780	Cabinet Utility Headboard	1952–1955	400–600	52
M781 on M771	Sculptura Dresser with Deck Top	1952–1953	650–850	49
M790	King Utility Headboard	1953–1954	400–600	53
M792	Sculptura 5-Drawer chest	1953–1959	450–650	46
M1110	Cadence Headboard	1955–1957	400–600	54
M1514-1525	Encore Mr. and Mrs. Dresser With Mirror	1956–1966	450–650	32
M1518	Encore Pier Chest /Nightstand	1956	175–250	37
M1520	Utility Headboard	1956–1966	100–200	53
M1528	Encore Nightstand	1956–1966	150–200	37
M1529-1525	Encore Triple Dresser with Mirror	1956–1966	700–900	31
M1536 on M1521	Encore Dresser with Tambour Utility Deck	1956	650–850	34

DINING ROOM FURNITURE

Chairs

Style #	Description	Years	Value	Page
C2794C	Arm Chair	1936–1941	150–200	57
C2794A	Side Chair	1936–1941	100–150	58
C3526A	Side Chair	1939–1940	100–150	59
C3535A	Side Chair	1939–1943	75–125	58
C3595C	Arm Chair	1940–1944	75–125	58
M151A	Side Chair	1950–1951	50–100	64
M152A	Side Chair	1947–1950	40–80	61
M154C	Arm Chair	1950–1955	150–200	63
M154A	Side Chair	1950–1955	100–150	63
M155A	Side Chair	1947–1950	75–125	60
M157C	Arm Chair	1947–1950	75–125	60
M157A	Side Chair	1947–1950	50–100	61
M549C	Arm Chair	1953–1966	100–150	66
M551A	Side Chair	1952–1955	40–80	65
M552A	Side Chair	1953–1955	50–100	66
M553C	Arm Chair	1950–1953	50–100	64
M553A	Side Chair	1950–1953	40–80	64
M554C	Arm Chair	1953–1955	75–125	66
M555C	Arm Chair	1950–1955	150–200	61
M555A	Side Chair	1950–1955	100–150	62
M556C	Arm Chair	1952–1954	75–125	65
M953C	Arm Chair	1954–1955	75–125	67
M953A	Side Chair	1954–1955	50–100	67
M1551A	Side Chair	1956-1966	40–80	68
M1552C	Arm Chair	1956	100–150	69
M1552A	Side Chair	1956	75–125	68
M1553C	Arm Chair	1956-1966	75–125	70
M1553A	Side Chair	1956-1966	50–100	70

Tables

Style #	Description	Years	Value	Page
C2932G	Large Extension	1936-1939	600–800	71
C3347G	Large Extension	1938-1939	350–450	72
C3955G	Small Extension	1941-1942	200–300	72
M165G	Large Extension	1947-1952	500–700	72
M166G	Gate Leg	1947-1955	350–450	88
M169G	Junior Extension	1950-1955	350–450	74
M189G	Junior Extension	1951-1955	400–500	76
M197G	Triple Pedestal	1948-1955	700–900	80
M394G	Service Wagon	1951-1952	450–650	91
M786G	Double Pedestal	1952-1955	450–650	84
M789G	Large Extension	1953-1955	500–700	75
M950G	Round extension	1954-1955	450–650	78
M989G	Harmonic extension	1954-1955	350–450	86
M1556G	Double Pedestal	1956-1961	450–650	87
M1558G	Junior Extension	1956-1966	350–450	77
M1568G	Round extension	1958-1959	450–650	79

Servers, Buffets, and China Closets

Style #	Description	Years	Value	Page
C3316 on C3317	Airflow China Closet	1937–1939	400–600	94
C3318	Airflow Buffet	1937–1939	400–600	93
C3348	Corner Cabinet	1938–1939	450–650	97
C3709	Buffet	1940–1942	500–700	93
M175 on M590	China Closet	1950–1955	350–450	95
M176	Corner Cabinet	1948–1955	600–800	97
M196W	Credenza with Desk Drawer	1950	550–750	98
M198 on M593	Large China Closet	1950–1955	700–900	97
M590	Server	1950–1955	200–300	95
M592	Buffet	1950–1955	250–350	96
M593	Credenza	1950–1955	400–600	96
M999 on M592	Buffet with China Top	1954–1955	400–600	96
M1543	Credenza	1956–1965	400–600	101
M1546 on M1542	Buffet with China Top	1956–1959	500–700	99
M1547 on M1543	Crown Glass China on Credenza	1956–1965	800–1000	100
M1547 on M1544	Crown Glass China on Credenza	1956–1965	800–1000	101
M1597	Server	1961–1966	200–300	101

LIVING ROOM FURNITURE

Seating

Style #	Description	Years	Value	Page
C3325C	Occasional Chair	1937–1940	150–200	116
C3326C	Barrel Chair	1937–1939	150–200	116
C3341RC	Right Arm Filler	1937–1938	200–300	110
C3341LC	Left Arm Filler	1937–1938	200–300	110
C3367–66	Davenport	1938–1939	800–1000	111
C3980C	Arm Chair	1941–1944	300–400	111
C3980-68	Davenport	1941–1944	800–1000	111
C3985C	Arm Chair	1941–1944	300–400	112
C3987–66	Davenport	1941–1944	800–1000	112
M340C	Pull-up Chair	1949–1952	150–200	117
M345C	Tub Chair	1950–1957	150–250	118
M355C	Arm Chair	1950–1953	300–400	114
M358-68	Davenport	1950–1953	800–1000	114
M360RC	Right Arm Filler	1947–1948	175–250	113
M360LC	Left Arm Filler	1947–1948	175–250	113
M363	Curved Filler	1947–1948	150–200	113
CM367LC	Aristo. Left Arm Filler	1950–1953	175–250	103
CM367RC	Aristo. Right Arm Filler	1950–1953	175–250	103
CM367	Aristo. Armless Filler	1950–1953	150–200	103
CM367C	Aristo. Arm Chair	1950–1953	350–450	104
CM367D	Aristo. Platform Rocker	1952–1953	500–700	105
CM368LC	Aristo. Left Arm Double Filler	1952–1953	300–400	105

Style #	Description	Years	Value	Page
CM388LC	Aristo. Left Arm Filler	1951–1953	225–275	106
CM388RC	Aristo. Right Arm Filler	1951–1953	225–275	106
CM388	Aristo. Armless Filler	1951–1953	150–225	106
CM388C	Aristo. Arm Chair	1951–1953	400–500	107
CM389-68	Aristo. Davenport	1952–1953	800–1000	106
M560C	Arm Chair	1951–1953	350–450	114
M568C	Open Arm Tub Chair	1951–1958	200–275	119
M569C	Pull-up Chair	1951–1959	150–200	119
M595C	Arm Chair	1954–1955	300–400	115
M596LC	Left Arm Double Filler	1954–1955	350–450	115
M596RC	Right Arm Double Filler	1954–1955	350–450	115
CM927C	Aristo. Arm Chair	1954–1966	350–450	109
CM929-66	Aristo. Davenport	1954–1966	800–1000	108
M1170C	Arm Chair	1955–1957	250–350	116

Occasional Tables

Style #	Description	Years	Value	Page
C2927G	End Table	1936–1938	100–200	131
C3170G	Step End Table	1936–1939	100–200	126
C3549G	Round Lamp Table	1939–1940	175–275	129
C3717G	Cocktail Table with Drawer	1940–1942	275–375	120
C3753G	Step End Table	1940–1944	150–250	126
C3962G	Oval End Table	1941–1942	150–250	132
M304G	Step End Table	1947–1949	150–250	127
M306G	Round Cocktail Table	1947–1955	200–300	120
M307G	Square Cocktail Table	1949–1952	300–400	121
M308G	Step End Table	1948–1953	75–150	127
M312G	Nesting Tables	1949–1953	400–600	135
M316G	Cocktail Table	1949	200–300	122
M319G	Cocktail Table	1949–1954	200–300	121
M335G	Cocktail Table	1950–1953	225–325	122
M337G	Lamp Table	1950–1953	150–250	130
M338G	Corner Table	1950–1953	200–300	134
M364G	Lamp Table	1950–1955	225–325	130
M391G	End Table	1950–1952	150–250	133
M392G	Square Cocktail Table	1950–1955	300–400	123
M393G	Center Table	1950–1952	300–400	131
M396G	Wedge Step End Table	1950–1953	100–200	128
M503G	Magazine End Table	1953–1957	175–275	133
M791G	End Table	1952–1953	125–225	133
M794G	Step End Table with Drawer	1953–1955	175–275	128
M795G	Large Cocktail Table	1953–1955	300–400	124
M902G	Nesting Tables	1954–1955	500–700	136
M905G	Cocktail Table with Drawer	1954–1955	400–500	125
M908G	Step End Table	1954–1955	100–200	129
CM970G	Aristo. Corner Table	1954–1955	100–200	134
M991G	Cocktail Table	1954–1955	200–300	124
M992G	End Table	1954–1955	150–250	115
M993G	Lamp Table	1954–1955	175–275	109
M1502G	End Table	1957–1966	150–250	134
M1505G	Large Cocktail Table	1957–1966	300–400	125
M1584G	Step End Table	1956–1957	100–200	129

Utility Pieces

Desks

Style #	Description	Years	Value	Page
C3539W	Crescendo Vanity/Desk	1939–1940	600–800	139
C3977W	Desk Bookcase	1941–1942	600–800	145
M320W	Kneehole Desk	1950–1965	800–1000	140
M327W	Table Desk	1950–1954	350–450	142
M328W	Desk Bookcase	1951–1954	700–900	145
M389W	Desk Chest	1952–1954	400–600	146
M783W	Student Desk	1952–1961	500–700	142
M926W	Vanity Desk	1954–1956	1000–1200	141
M1575W	Princess Desk	1964–1965	900–1100	143

Miscellaneous Storage

Style #	Description	Years	Value	Page
C2925G	Pivot Top Console	1936–1938	300–400	155
C2929X	Compartment Bookcase	1937–1938	250–350	149
C3544	Crescendo Pier Chest	1939–1940	350–450	148
M177	Tambour Front Chest	1947–1948	500–700	152
M178	Tambour Front Chest	1947–1948	600–800	151
M179	Tambour Utility Case	1949–1954	400–600	153
M313G	Pivot Top Console	1951–1952	300–400	156
M321	Straight Bookcase	1947–1965	200–300	147
M322	Corner Bookcase	1947–1961	300–400	147
M326	Cabinet Bookcase	1952–1961	300–400	148
M395	Record Cabinet	1951–1952	500–700	150
M505 on M504	Room Divider	1953–1956	1600–2000	157
M526	Utility Cabinet	1952–1953	350–450	149
M528	Encore Pier Chest	1952–1954	350–450	150